Tumultuous

Y.R. Perry

Copyright © 2018 by Y.R. Perry

All rights reserved. This book or any portion thereof may not be reproduced or used in any manner whatsoever without the express written permission of the publisher except for the use of brief quotations in a book review.

Printed in the United States of America

First Printing, 2018

For information, write:

yperry92@gmail.com

Dedication

This book is dedicated to inspire my son, Jermaine, and my daughter, Catawna, to exhaust every talent God has instilled in them no matter what it is, no matter the naysayers.
To always think Rich thoughts, talk Rich talk, and make
Rich moves.
God Is Watching and the universe is listening.

~ a talent not acted upon awaits a gravestone~

Acknowledgments

Editor: Marvin Cloud

Book Cover Design: Keith Crear of Grizzly Media

Self Published

CHAPTER 1
PAROLED FROM HELL

I can't believe this, not again. How could he? Yvette asked herself as her heart beat fast. Hyperventilation consumed her and she soon became disoriented. This wasn't a normal feeling. The stress and depression finally caught up with her. She made her way to the phone and as much as she hated to call her husband, Lawrence, he was the only family she had in Florida. She had moved away to support him in his career as a lieutenant for the police department. This was her second move. First she moved away from her family in California. Then she went to Georgia. Now Florida.

"I feel like I'm having a heart attack," Yvette said to Lawrence, barely able to hold the phone to her mouth.

"I'm on my way," Lawrence replied. He made it to their home in no time flat and took Yvette to the local hospital in Tampa. He dropped her off at the front entrance while he parked the car. Yvette walked in and attempted to check herself into the hospital. The nurse on duty could see she was confused and appeared in distressed. She immediately retrieved a wheelchair and took her to the back. The ER nurse looked at her, asked her a few questions, and determined she was having an anxiety attack.

"Miss Wells, you will be fine. Have you been under any extreme stress lately?" the doctor on duty asked. He was quite concerned.

Yvette laid on the gurney and looked at Lawrence. He held her hand and pretended to be the best husband in the world. He was poised and polished as though he was the picture of perfection. His uniform was pressed and his badge shined like a light. If looks could stop a heart from beating, the staff would need a code blue for Yvette. Lawrence's eyes and Yvette's eyes met. The tension was extreme between them.

"I will come back in a few minutes to check on you. We want you to stay here for an hour or so for observation to see how the medication works," the doctor stated.

"Thank you, doctor," Yvette replied softly.

******

"Thank you, Jesus!" Yvette uttered in complete exhaustion as she crossed the state line into Texas. We made it kiddos!"

Yvette looked over at her daughter, Katrina, and then turned into her rear-view mirror and looked at her son, Jaden. He was nestled in the backseat among some of the items she packed from the house that would not fit in her trunk. The divorce was set in motion. The only thing left to do was wait on the final documents to be mailed and she would be a free woman once again. She would be free from the lies, deceit, and the hurt no one could stand. This was her second time trying to save her marriage and much to her dismay, nothing about Lawrence had changed. He was still a cheat. Being a lieutenant on the police force made it easy for him to attract a lot of women. After all, women love a man in uniform, right? Yvette had to admit as his soon-to-be-ex, that was one of the things that turned her on.

"Mom, I need to go to the restroom!" exclaimed Katrina. "How far is it before we get to Aunt Kelsey's house?" She wiggled her legs in an effort to hold her bladder.

"We still have quite a ways to go." Yvette was tired. "We will stop at the gas station up ahead."

"I thought you said we were in Texas," Jaden remarked, as he sat upright.

"We are in Texas, but we still have a ways before we get into Austin," Yvette explained, as she pulled into the gas station right off the next exit. Jaden and Katrina barely allowed the car to stop before flinging open the doors and jumping out to stretch their legs and race to the restroom. Yvette followed behind them in a slow pace. She was weary from the long drive. With every step she struggled to keep her legs from cramping.

"Finally I'm free," she said as she took a deep breath. "It is over. Now, it's time to start my new life." Jaden and Katrina came out of the restrooms. "Come on children, grab a couple of snacks and let's get back on the road to Kelsey's house. I want to get the keys to our new place before it gets too late."

While dealing with her divorce in California, Yvette's sister, Kelsey, worked with a REALTOR® in Texas to help Yvette secure a home. She wanted her own space when she got in town. Yvette had moved back home to be around her family while going through the transition with her husband. But, she decided she needed a complete change of scenery.

"I don't want anything else to drink," Katrina said. "I will just get some potato chips. I don't want to stop and go to the restroom again."

"Okay, get what you're going to get and let's go!" Yvette commanded.

They finally made it to Kelsey's house.

"Let's go and grab the keys and get to our new home."

The trio walked up to Kelsey's front door and knocked.

"Hey Aunt Kelsey," Jaden and Katrina said.

"Hey, guys!" Kelsey said with excitement. "I'm glad you all made it safely. Oh my gosh, Yvette, you look as if you've been run over by two trucks!" Kelsey chuckled. She paused for a second. "You smell."

"Girl, you try driving for three days through the desert with two children in the summer time, jumping in and out of the car for bathroom breaks, snacks, and quick naps in between."

"You are really serious about getting away from him this time, huh?" Kelsey was concerned. "I can't believe you guys spent $20000 on a celebration to renew your vows and rededicate your life to each other after everything he did, only for you to leave three months later. Kelsey expressed in disbelief.

"You know there are some things that money can't buy and there are also some people that will never change no matter what. I tried everything I could. I accepted some things, I forgave some things, I changed some things about me until I almost lost me, mentally and physically. Once I got to that level, I knew it was time to go." Yvette had a blank look on her face as though she was reliving every horrible moment. She changed the subject. "Girl, do you have the keys to the house? Did you do a walk-through and check everything?"

"Yeah, everything is good."

"Okay, hand them over. We're going to head over and get these air mattresses set up so we can get some rest."

"So, you're not going to shower? You just going to leave here funky, huh?" Kelsey laughed.

"Girl, I will shower when I get to the house and get settled. I'm not getting out anywhere. I have gas in the car and I'm going straight there. Besides, who cares? I'm not trying to impress anyone."

"You never know where your king may be. You have to stay ready ... look your best at all times." Kelsey flipped her hair and stuck out her large boobs with her hands on her hips like a model.

"Girl stop," Yvette chuckled. "I will see you in the morning for breakfast. Let's go, Jaden and Katrina. I'm tired." They loaded into the car and drove off to their new home for a new beginning. After a short drive they arrived at the address.

"Wow, it's kind of dark out here, Mom," Katrina said. She was concerned.

"Yeah, I guess the real estate agent forgot to turn on a porch light. It's fine. We just need to get in and get some sleep."

Yvette opened the door and much to her dismay, the house looked nothing on the inside like it did on the real estate agent's website. Even the children were shocked. They were used to the fancy neighborhoods and houses that a lifetime of marriage provided.

"We're going to make the best of it," Yvette said. "It's ours."

She thought, *That's the last time I will trust family to do a walk-through on a house.*

The next day, the movers brought the furniture. Jaden and Katrina began to decorate their rooms and everything started to come together. The sun was bright. It confirmed this would be a beautiful new beginning.

Yvette coordinated everything while dressed in moving attire: cut-off denim shorts, tennis shoes, a bandanna on her head and a shirt emblazoned with the words, "No Stress." The doorbell rang and Yvette raced downstairs with a box in her hand.

"Who is it?" she asked.

"Girl, open the door. You know I was coming to help you!" Kelsey shouted, "Who else could it be knocking at your door?" Yvette swung the door open.

"You said you would be here at 9 a.m. It's now noon. You missed breakfast."

"Oh. Better late than never," she smirked. "Elisha came to help, too."

Where is she?"

"Girl, she's in the car trying to schedule a booty call ." Yvette laughed loudly.

"Girl come on, let's get this over with!" Kelsey shouted at the car where Elisha sat.

"I'm coming!" Elisha shouted as she flung the door open. "You know I have to make sure I have the D on Deck at all times." She made her way to the front door.

"Girl, is that all you think about?" Kelsey asked and rolled her eyes.

Elisha paused for a minute. "For the most part, yes." She laughed hysterically. "Let me see, first thing in the morning, right before lunch, and if I'm in bed alone at night, I guess you could say so."

"Girl, get in here," Yvette laughed as she held the door open.

"Oh, my God. I hate unpacking!" Yvette exclaimed. She sat in the middle of the floor; boxes surrounded her like mountains.

"Come on, let's get this done," Kelsey said. "These boxes are not going to unpack themselves."

"Right!" Elisha stated. "You got me for two hours max, maybe three. I have things to do and besides we need to get out later so you can see what the city has to offer."

"Girl, I hope you are not talking about men," Yvette said with dismay. "I am not interested. The only thing I'm interested in from this city is a great job, great schools for Jaden and Katrina, and great food. Men are the furthest thing from my mind. It's too soon."

"Give her some time," Kelsey said.

"Time!" Elisha shouted. "The only way to get over a man is to get under a new one." Kelsey and Yvette looked at each other and laughed. "Y'all laughing but I speak the truth and nothing but the truth. Now, come on. Let's hurry up. There's new men to be met and a past to be forgotten."

CHAPTER 2
DECOMPRESSION

Later that night, Yvette's phone rang.

"Hello?" Yvette said groggily.

"Bitch, I know you lying. You better not be sleep!" Elisha exclaimed.

"What? I'm tired."

"Girl, Kelsey and I are on our way there. You better be ready."

From the background, Kelsey said, "Let her rest if she needs to."

"Rest is for the old and the weary, that of which you are neither," Elisha stated.

"Oh my gosh, really Elisha?" Yvette asked.

"Yes, really! We are on our way, so get it in gear. No moping in the great state of Texas. There's way too much to do and when I say 'do,' I mean men."

Yvette shook her head. "All right, all right. I'm getting dressed. I will be done in about an hour."

"Chop-chop chic. Let's get it!"

******

"Club Ambience huh? Is this where you wanted to bring me so badly?" Yvette asked.

"Honey child, this is the spot where all the ballers hang out," Elisha responded with excitement. Her eyes were all aglow like a kid on Christmas morning.

"Girl, stop it! This place is full of perpetrators ... guys who rent cars and jewelry for the weekend to impress women," Kelsey laughed. The trio got out of the car and made their way to the club's entrance.

A patio was off to the side where people could enjoy the night air, smoke a cigar or relax under the night sky while listening to the music from inside. Yvette looked around timidly. The scene was definitely different from anything she was used to as the wife of a police lieutenant. She hadn't seen the inside of a club in years. The name "Ambience" fit the bill. Everything was white and red with black and gold trim. There were white leather seating sections and white bar stools at the bar with red lighting and strobe lights flashing everywhere to the beat of the music. Crystal chandeliers adorned the ceilings and were strategically placed throughout the club to create the ultimate atmosphere. The energy, look, and dress, screamed "grown and sexy." Yvette gave herself a once-over to make sure she fit into the category.

"You okay?" Kelsey asked. "Girl, you look like a deer caught in headlights. Loosen up. It's okay."

"Yes, please, you is free now ma'am. This here bees freedom, yes it is," Elisha mocked.

"Stop! You guys know it's been a minute for me," Yvette said coyly.

"Here's to you coming out of retirement. Drink this," Elisha handed her a drink. Don't ask any questions just drink.

Yvette took a sip. "Mmmmm, this tastes pretty good."

The night wore on and after a couple of drinks, Yvette finally let go and began to breathe. She danced to the music and scanned the room. She saw many great looking guys. She had not looked at men that way in a long time. She only had eyes for her husband, and then it hit her. *I am really single, I can do whatever I want and whoever I want when I want. I'm going to enjoy my life.* A smile came over her face and in that moment, she let it all go. She rocked her hips from side to side in a circular motion, and her tight, form-fitting red dress showed off her wide ample hips, thick thighs, and plump derriere. All rested upon a pair of six- inch strapped stilettos. Long black hair loosely curled, adorned her shoulders. The lights of the club shimmered over her body and illuminated her dark-skinned. She was indeed free and she danced like she was liberated.

"All right now!" Elisha shouted over the music. "Don't hurt nobody."

The night continued, the music got better, and the drinks kept coming. Although there were fine guys of all shapes, sizes, and colors, Yvette's only interest was emotional release and having a great time, unlike what Elisha had in mind. Kelsey was in the midst of a separation and trying to get over her cheating husband by dating someone she had fallen crazy in love with. He lived with his children's mother. Elisha was married but her and her husband had this unspoken relationship. He slept with whomever he wanted and so did she. They never spoke about it, as long as the two respected each other and never let the outside cross over into the inside

It started to get late and Yvette was tired. Kelsey sat at the table with her head down. She fell asleep after one drink. Elisha was stashed off in a dark corner talking to a tall caramel-skin guy with a swagger that said he sold big time drugs. He was most definitely her type. Yvette made her way over to her.

"Girl, it's time to go! Kelsey is over there asleep on the table and I'm tired. It's almost 1:30."

"Okay," Elisha said. She was aggravated. "Here are the keys. I will meet you in the car. That's why I normally roll solo."

"Girl, the club is about to close. Are you serious?" Yvette yelled.

She went over to the table where Kelsey rested her head. She tapped her on the shoulder and they proceeded to leave the club. Before they left, Yvette had to see what was happening on the patio. There was as much going on outside as inside. She scanned the area not looking for anything or anyone in particular. As she walked away she felt a tug at her hand.

She turned around and a guy asked, "You leaving already?"

He was a smooth dark-skinned guy who stood about 6 foot 2 inches with a freshly-edged tapered haircut and nicely trimmed goatee. He looked like he had stepped out of a celebrity barber shop. He had on Gucci shades, a white button-down shirt and blue jeans. He had a swagger so mean it was hard to be offended by him approaching her that way.

Yvette replied, "I've been here all night. Where were you earlier?"

With a deep tone and southern drawl, he responded, "Watching you."

"Oh, really?" she smirked. "Why are you wearing those shades? It's dark out. Are you cockeyed and trying to hide it?"

"No, I'm not cockeyed," he chuckled. He removed his shades.

Yvette noticed something that was as shocking as being cockeyed. His smile lit up the room. Not because his teeth were gleaming white, but he had a mouth full of gold teeth. Yvette's eyes grew wide. She was disappointed. She was a California girl and this was something she didn't see often except on TV. This was on her "I would never date a guy who has" list.

She forced a smile and said, "Okay so you're not cockeyed. What's your name?"

"Geo."

"I'm Yvette. Nice to meet you, Geo."

"Since you're leaving, can I call you later?" he asked.

"I'll tell you what, why don't you give me your number and I will call you?"

"That's cool," Geo spoke confidently.

Yvette pulled out her phone and put Geo's number in it.

"I hope to hear from you," he smiled.

"I'm going to call you," she said.

In the back of her mind she thought, *I'm not going to call this dude ever. I mean he's cute but he looks like some swagged out dope dealer. I wouldn't be able to take him to any corporate functions. People will look at me like I'm crazy!*

"Come on!" Kelsey yelled. "I'm tipsy as hell and I am sleepy."

"Okay. I got to go. I will call you," she said as she stepped off the patio into the parking lot. Elisha finally made her way to the car and they began their drive home.

"He's not answering my calls!" Kelsey fumed from the back seat. "I'm feeling some type of way and I want to see him. He must be in bed with his baby mama and not out tonight otherwise he would answer. I have called him like five times! That's the only reason I came out tonight. We were going to get a room after I left the club, but that bastard has lied. I know he's with her!" Kelsey sobbed.

"Girl, give me the phone. Let me call him and see if he answers," Yvette said. She dialed the number but she didn't get an answer. "I'm going to leave him a message."

"Yes, leave him a message!" Kelsey yelled from the back seat in a drunken stupor and through tears.

"I know you see my sister calling you!" Yvette shouted into the phone. "You got her all sad thinking she was going to see you tonight."

"Yeah, you must be with your baby mama!" Kelsey got louder.

"You bitches are stupid! Hang up that phone." Elisha stated.

"Why do you think I do what I do? They don't give a damn, why should we?"

"But I love him!" Kelsey cried.

"Girl, if you don't shut your drunk ass up!" Elisha burst out in laughter. Yvette did also.

"Yeah she's good and drunk. You know it doesn't take nothing but a teaspoon of alcohol in a glass of water and she's gone," Yvette chuckled.

"Y'all don't understand," Kelsey sobbed loudly. "The sex is so good. He's better than my husband. He makes me feel ...."Then all of a sudden there was silence.

"Feel what?" Yvette and Elisha asked simultaneously. They looked in the back seat and Kelsey was asleep. Yvette and Elisha looked at each other and laughed.

"That dick will drive you crazy," Elisha said.

"Yeah," Yvette sighed. "It will also keep you in situations you should and could have walked away from."

******

The next morning, Yvette's phone rang.

"Girl you sleep," the voice on the phone asked.

"What time is it?" Yvette asked. She realized it was Elisha on the other end.

"It's almost noon. How much did you drink last night? Kelsey told me you were booed up last night with some guy."

"I wouldn't say booed up. Some guy stopped me on the way to the car but he's not my type."

"What was wrong with him?"

"His mouth is full of bling is what's wrong."

"Honey, there's a lot of guys here in Texas that have grills but most of them are removable and just for show."

"Girl, I pray so, because you know I work in corporate. How am I going to show up to a company party and picnics with him smiling, blinding people, and them judging him thinking he's some sort of drug dealer before they get a chance to know him?"

"It sounds like you have already judged him yourself without getting to know him so you're no different. At least call him and get to know him for yourself. You never know."

"Girl, I guess," Yvette sighed.

"So, what's up for tonight?"

"Girl, nothing. I'm going to stay in tonight and pace myself on this going out thing. You know I'm new to this ... being married for 15 years and not going to the club at all or going every blue moon with my husband. I have kind of gotten out of the swing of it."

"Honey, you better get back into the swing of it. I told you, you is free now."

"Your ass is crazy, Elisha," Yvette laughed.

"I will but at my pace. I have plenty of time. I need to get settled into this life."

"I guess I understand. If you change your mind, call me. I will probably already be out and about anyway."

"Okay, will do. I will talk to you later."

With still a lot of unpacking to do, Yvette looked around the room. Boxes were still packed high. She took a deep breath and begin unpacking and sorting boxes by rooms.

She turned on the TV and watched music videos and listened to the music to keep her motivated while she unpacked.

She thought, *I would have had so much more done had I stayed in last night. Oh, well, these boxes are not going to unpack themselves and the kids don't get home 'till 4.*

She cranked up the volume on the TV and let the music videos play. One video in particular featured rappers with gold teeth. This was new to Yvette but it made her think about that guy, Geo, she met at Club Ambience.

Maybe I am being a tad bit judgmental. Maybe I should give him a call and see what his conversation is like.

She scrolled through the list of contacts on her phone, located his number, and dialed it.

"Hello?" Geo answered. His voice was semi-deep with a southern twang.

"May I speak to Geo?" she asked.

"This is him," Geo replied.

"Hi, this is Yvette, the girl you met the other night at Club Ambience. How are you doing?"

"I was hoping I would hear from you. I wasn't sure. You seem so cold and in a hurry."

"I was in a hurry. I haven't been in town long and my sister and my cousin, got me in the streets already and I haven't had time to regroup and adjust to my new surroundings."

"I can understand that."

"So when am I going to see you again? And I'm not taking no for an answer."

"What?" Yvette laughed.

"I said when am I going to see you again and I'm not taking no for an answer," Geo repeated.

"I think we should talk on the phone more so I can get to know you a little better first. I mean you got all these gold teeth in your mouth, you dress nice, but you might be some kind of drug dealer or gang banger."

"Why would you say that?" Geo laughed. "Because I have gold teeth? I got these when I was young, you know, not thinking."

Oh, my damn! Yvette thought to herself. *It's not a removable grill, they are permanent.* "Oh, okay."

"So what are you doing tonight?" Geo asked.

"I'm not doing anything until I get my house organized. No more clubbing or dates until then or I will never get done."

"I understand, but that will be the first and last no I will accept from you," he replied in a cocky tone.

"Excuse me?" Yvette asked with a smile in her voice.

"You heard me. I will let you go so you can get done and not have an excuse to tell me no again.

"Okay" she replied with a laugh. "I will talk to you later."

"I hope so," he said charmingly.

Yvette hung up the phone and immediately called Elisha. There wasn't an answer. She then called Kelsey.

"Hello?" Kelsey answered.

"Girl, guess what? The guy I met last night has permanent gold teeth! I was praying that they were a grill as you guys say but they are in there for good!"

"He must have got those back in the day. Most guys here have grills that they can put in for show and take them out when they don't want to have them anymore."

"Well, that's not the case."

"Okay, besides that, Judgmental Judy, how was his conversation?"

"I don't know. I haven't quite got around to asking him a whole lot about himself. He wants to see me again, I'm just not sure."

"What if he's a really good guy?"

"I don't know. I got to get past the gold teeth."

"Okay, girl, let me finish unpacking. It seems like I will never get done. I just had to call someone once I found out."

"Try and get to know him first. We women are quick to judge. You never know, he may be a diamond in the rough."

"Yeah, okay." Yvette hung up the phone and started the tiring task of unpacking and putting things in their designated places. She heard the front door open while she was in the kitchen.

"Jaden, Katrina, is that you?"

"Yes ma'am, it's me, Jaden."

"How was your first day at the new school?"

"It was okay."

"Start unpacking your room and organizing it. Your sister should be home shortly to do the same. I'm going to finish unpacking the kitchen so I can cook you guys dinner."

"Okay," Jaden answered and went up the stairs.

Shortly thereafter, Katrina came home and was instructed to do the same. Later that evening, once Yvette got all the kitchen items unpacked and in place, she cooked her first meal in their new house. Dinner consisted of baked chicken, homemade mac and cheese, (Jayden's favorite) and green beans with dinner rolls (Katrina's favorite).

As Yvette sat at the table she looked at her two children, took a deep breath and exhaled.

It's finally over she thought. *No more mental, or physical abuse, no more lies and cheating, no more having nowhere to run to or anyone to take my side. I'm free of a hell that was once called a marriage. No more of his erratic behavior and his boss covering up for him. No more extravagant gifts and trips to try to bandage the pain and mental anguish.*

It felt like the weight of the world had been lifted from her shoulders and the knots in her stomach began to loosen. She felt free indeed.

CHAPTER 3
TRYING SOMETHING NEW

She had almost gotten her room organized. It was the last one to be unpacked. She sat in the middle of the floor on the light cream-colored Berber carpet, listening to old school slow jams, from Gerald Levert, Guy, Toni Tony Tone, and R Kelly to help her get through the monotonous unpacking process. Elisha called.

"Hey, girl what's up?"

"Child, I heard about your thugaboo with the permanent gold teeth," she laughed hysterically. "Sounds more like my type not yours."

"Yeah, I know right?" Yvette replied.

"He may be a very nice guy. Don't judge a book by its cover. He told you it was something he did at a younger time in his life. Girl, you know they didn't start making pull out grills until recently. Give him at least one date and see what he's talking about."

"I may just do that. You know I may need a Lil Thug in my life. Try a little something new for a change. I mean I am single to mingle. Why not?"

"Okay! That's what I'm talking about. Keep me posted."

Later, that night Geo called.

"What are you up to?"

"Oh, nothing, lounging around for a minute before I head to happy hour with the girls," she replied.

"I need to see you and I'm not taking no for an answer."

"I already have plans with the girls!"

"Let's meet up somewhere before you head out. I want

to see you for a few minutes, then you can be on your way. Maybe I will beat your girls to the punch next time."

"I guess I can do that as long as you don't try to kidnap me," she laughed.

"Naah, I'm not going to kidnap you," he laughed, "but you might want me to." He was confident as usual

Later that evening, Yvette got dressed to meet Elisha and Kelsey at a popular happy hour spot she was told had the best wings, drinks, and the hottest guys, not to mention the drinks and wings were 25 cents for Wing Wednesday. She turned on music to get her hyped to party. Mostly it was Beyoncé mixed with Lil Wayne.

Her selection of attire for the evening was a pair of form-fitting dark jeans that accentuated her curvaceous hips, small waist, and nice firm round ass. Her shirt of choice was a white baby T-shirt with the words "Bebe" stitched on it with rhinestones across her chest. She wore a pair of carmel-colored wedges that matched the stitching in her jeans. Her 18-inch black Brazilian flat iron hair laid silky down her back. Her lashes and makeup were beat to the Gods.

She set out to meet Geo. They agreed to meet in the parking lot of a local restaurant that was along the way. Yvette pulled into a parking space and picked up her phone to let Geo know she was there.

"Hey, where are you?" she asked.

"I will be pulling up in one minute," he replied.

"Okay. Hurry, this is my first time at this spot and I want to get there with my girls so I don't have to walk in alone."

"I'm pulling up in a minute, I promise. When you see me, you might change your mind and want to stay with me."

"I doubt that. I don't know you like that."

"I just pulled into the parking lot," Geo said. "Where are you? I'm in a red car."

Yvette looked up to see a red Mercedes Benz candy painted red on chrome rims with dark, tinted windows looking as though it was fresh off a showroom floor. *Oh my God,* she thought to herself, *this dude is definitely a drug dealer.*

"I'm in a silver Nissan Altima."

Geo got out of the car, wearing a white T-shirt, pressed Levi's and white Forces. He had a fresh haircut and wore those same Gucci shades he had on that night at the club. He also had on bling from his wrist to his neck, ears, and teeth. *Yep, he's got to be a dope dealer, but he sure looks good.* He was made up of all of her weaknesses.

He leaned into her car window and asked, "Are you going to get out?"

Yvette stepped out of the car and Geo slowly gave her a once-over from head to toe. "I see you got your get one jeans on," he smiled.

"Get one?" Yvette asked. She was puzzled.

"Yeah, those jeans are definitely going to get you one of whatever it is you want tonight."

She laughed. "I have never heard that one before."

"Yeah, you look damn good," he said.

"Thanks," she smiled.

"I'm not going to hold you up, I just wanted to see your face. I haven't seen you since the club. Can I get a hug before you go?" he asked.

"Sure, but don't try to rub on my ass," she joked.

"I wouldn't do that. I'm a gentleman," he smiled. Lights from the parking lot bounced off his gold teeth. *Oh, my goodness this is so not for me,* she thought. She step closer to him to initiate the hug and put her arms around his neck as he grabbed her and wrapped his arms firmly around her waist. The smell of his cologne was intoxicating and arousing at the same time. Her gut told her nothing good could come out of this, but her mind said, *Take a walk on the wild side for a change. You have played good girl for almost 20 years and all it got you was lied to, cheated on, mentally and physically abused. You're in charge now.* She decided right then and there this was not the last time she would see Geo.

"I got to go."

"Okay. Be careful with all that precious cargo." He smiled like a sly fox.

"Boy stop!" Yvette jumped in her car and headed to the sports bar to meet Kelsey and Elisha. Her phone rang.

"Bitch, where you at?" Elisha shouted. "We are in the parking lot waiting on you."

"I'm about five minutes away," Yvette replied.

"We're going to go ahead and go in and get a table before it gets packed. Call us when you get to the door and one of us will come get you. We know how you don't like walking through crowds by yourself."

Yvette pulled into the parking lot of the sports bar and like Elisha said, it was packed. There weren't any free spaces to park, therefore, Yvette used the valet service. She called Elisha to let her know to meet her at the door. It was jam-packed inside and on the patio. The DJ blared music, drinks flowed and Hookah smoke hung in the air. Kelsey met her.

"Hey, girl."

"Hey, chick," Yvette replied and gave her a hug.

"Damn, it's crowded in here."

They parted their way through the crowd to a table in the far left corner.

"Bitch what happened to you? Did you get lost? You left before I did and this place is not far from your house," Elisha said playfully.

"And hello to you, too," Yvette responded with a chuckle and gave her a friendly kiss on the cheek.

"If you must know, I stopped to meet up with Geo for a minute. He wanted to meet with me since we hadn't seen each other in the flesh since that night."

"Hmmmm," Elisha smirked. "How was it?"

"Girl!" Yvette exclaimed. She took a deep breath, closed her eyes and put her hand on her chest as though she was reminiscing. "He pulled up in a candy red painted Benz on chrome and hopped out looking just as nice and smelling even better. I hugged him before I left and the smell of his cologne almost made me have an orgasm."

"Damn, you look like you're about to have one now. Calm down before you wet your panties. We just got here," Elisha said. They all laughed hysterically.

As the day turned into night the music was great, the wings were the best, and the atmosphere was phenomenal.

There were all sorts of guys. Yvette gave her number to a few but she couldn't stop thinking about Geo.

He was different from any guy she had ever dated, and definitely one she said she would never date, but the unknown made her curious. Besides, look where her so-called type had gotten her. A string of broken relationships and a marriage of misery that ended in a long, drawn-out, and horrible divorce.

The next day, she couldn't get the thought of him and the smell of his cologne off her mind. She called him. There wasn't an answer. A few minutes later her phone rang and it was Geo.

"Hey, beautiful, I'm sorry I missed your call. I was taking care of some business. How was your night out?" he asked.

"It was nice. I had a good time," she replied.

"I'm sure you had dudes all over you."

"Naah," she laughed. "I wouldn't say all that."

"You're not going to tell me the truth anyways. What are you doing later on? It's my turn now and it's early so I know no one has called and made plans with you." Yvette paused.

"I really wanted to chill out today and not do anything."

"Yeah? You can chill with me. Nothing major. My brother is doing a little barbecue at his house, just him and his girl and a few friends." Geo said.

"Hmmmmm..." Yvette started.

"I will settle for a slow yes instead of a fast no."

Yvette thought of their first meeting and decided meeting his brother and his friends would possibly give her a better idea of who he was.

"Okay," she responded.

"It's a date," Geo replied, as if he already knew there wasn't any way she would say no. "Let's meet in the same parking lot of the restaurant where we first met. You can leave your car there and ride with me. It will be okay because the restaurant doesn't close until 1 a.m."

"Are you sure my car will be safe? I don't want to come back and it has been towed." Yvette was concerned.

"Don't worry and if it does, I got you," he responded.

That evening, Yvette met Geo in the parking lot as discussed. He got out of the car and opened the door for her to get in. *Possible bad boy but a gentleman* she thought. A dangerous combination.

"You're looking good," he said with a smile. "I see you're wearing heels. You know it's just a barbecue, right?"

"I know you said it was a barbecue but I always wear some type of heels and besides these are wedges. For the most part I'm always in heels unless I'm working out."

"Oh, I'm not complaining. Trust me," he said with a smile. He gave her a once-over as usual. On the drive to his brother's house, he played a number of slow jams, ranging from R&B to Neo-Soul. It wasn't exactly what Yvette expected. She had prepared herself to hear some sort of rap music, perhaps Jay-Z to Lil Wayne. *Maybe I have wrongfully prejudged him.* The drive wasn't long, maybe about 20 minutes. Before going into the house, Geo stopped to talk to two guys who were standing outside.

"Hold on a minute," he told Yvette. "I need to holla at them for a minute."

Yvette sat in the car while he got out and talked to them. She took notice of her surroundings. People hung out in the garage while music blared. Some of the men wore white t-shirts with sagging pants and some wore baseball caps. The women wore short shorts or short dresses. Some of them wore tennis shoes and others wore heels, hair weave, and eye lashes for days, not to mention there were children everywhere.

She turned her head to see if she could hear the conversation between Geo and the guys he had to talk to before going in. She could vaguely hear him say, "Did you count the money?"

One of the guys was tall and fair-skinned with braids. He said, "Yeah, I did."

"Okay. Now, I need you to go and drop half off at the spot and I will meet up with you later."

Yvette's stomach turned into knots and she immediately became nervous. *Oh, my God I was right. What have I gotten myself into?* Her heart sank and she didn't know what to do. She didn't know where she was, and she didn't have a family member or friend nearby. She started to formulate a plan. *I'm going to tell him I feel sick and need to go home. No, I'm going to tell him the kids called and something is going on at the house. Yeah, that's what I will say.* She could see Geo headed back towards the car as she looked in the passenger mirror.

He opened her door and asked, "You ready?"

Before he could say another word, she looked into his eyes, saw his freshly cut and tapered haircut, his neatly trimmed goatee surrounding those luscious lips on that chocolate skin with that 1000 kilowatt smile and all the nervousness left her body. She got out of the car and approached the house with Geo. This was not her type of barbecue, at least the other guests were not her type. Yvette found a corner in the backyard where a chair was by itself. She sat there.

The women at the party seemed to know each other. She could see them giving her the side eye, trying to figure out who she was and wondering why she was being antisocial. Yvette didn't care, she was there with Geo and that's all that mattered. Geo got up and moved around from time to time, greeting friends and relatives, laughing and talking, but always checking to make sure she was okay.

"Do you want something to eat or drink?" Geo asked. Yvette first thought was to say no because she didn't eat just anybody's food, but then she thought, *hell, I'm already sitting here looking bougie and anti-social. I don't want them to think I'm too good to eat the food,* too.

"Sure," Yvette responded. Geo went to get her some food. A woman walked towards her.

"You smoke?" the woman asked while she held a marijuana blunt between her fingers.

"No, thanks," Yvette replied.

"Oh, okay. I'm Tammy, Ron's girlfriend. He's Geo's brother."

"Nice to meet you," Yvette said.

"Come sit over here with us. You don't have to sit alone."

"Okay." Yvette grabbed her purse and walked with Tammy to a group of ladies who were sitting and playing cards.

"Hey y'all, this is Geo's new girlfriend. I'm sorry, what's your name?" Tammy turned to her and asked.

"My name is Yvette," she replied, "but I'm not his girl. I'm just a friend."

"She don't smoke," Tammy stated.

"You play cards?" One of the ladies asked.

"Not really," Yvette responded.

"Damn, you don't smoke. You don't play cards. Geo got him a good-girl type on his hands," said a heavy set lady wearing a short tapered haircut, dyed blonde. She was loud and obnoxious. She laughed and so did the rest of the ladies at the table. Yvette saw Geo looking for her, plate in hand.

"Excuse me ladies," she said and walked towards him. "I'm over here," she said.

Geo handed her a plate with barbecue sausage, chicken, ribs, and two slices of bread. Yvette looked under the bread. She was puzzled. Something was missing.

"What's wrong? Why are you looking at the food like that?" Geo asked.

"Where are the sides? You know like baked beans, potato salad, etc?"

"Oh, we just throw meat on the grill and drink."

Yvette laughed. "I have never been to a barbecue where there was just meat and no sides." Nevertheless she rolled up a sausage link inside of a piece of bread and began to eat. The evening wore on and Geo continued to be attentive to Yvette. He made sure she was comfortable, fed her ribs off his plate, and danced with her. After a few drinks, she forgot all about the unsavory characters that surrounded her. This man had her attention and she had his.

"You about ready to go?" Geo asked. It was getting late. "Yeah. I'm a little tipsy. It's time for me to call it a night." Geo grabbed her by her hand and walked her to the car. "Go ahead and get in. I'm going to go say bye to my brother and let him know I'm leaving."

Five minutes later, he came back to the car and they drove to the restaurant where she had parked her car. Although tipsy and charmed by Geo's swagger and his personality, she couldn't get over the conversation she overheard. She wanted to ask him about it badly, but couldn't find the words. Geo popped in a CD, turned to Yvette and said, "Listen to the words in this song." The song began to play.

It was "Sweet Lady" by R&B singer, Tyrese. Yvette's stomach filled with butterflies and her heart fluttered. She felt like a schoolgirl on her first date. As he sang along, every so often he would reach over and grab her chin and turn her face toward him so that she would look at him. She turned away bashfully. They pulled into the parking lot. Geo got out of the car and opened the door for Yvette.

"Thanks for hanging out with me. Can I have a hug?"
"Of course," Yvette said. The two embraced tightly body to body. The smell of his cologne was all over his neck. Yvette inhaled deeply with her arms wrapped tightly around his neck. A wave of heat took over her body and she had erotic thoughts of him throwing her against his car and kissing her passionately, and saying, *I know what you need, don't be shy about it. I can tell it's been a minute for you. Let me put something on your mind for tonight.* Of course, none of that happened. The hug ended and he opened her car door to let her in, and didn't even give her as much as a kiss on the cheek.

"Call me and let me know you made it home safely. Are you sure you're okay to drive?"

"Yes, I'm fine." On her way home she turned the AC up an extra notch to cool her hormones. Geo had indeed sparked a flame down below that she had every intention of letting him extinguish.

CHAPTER 4
IT'S ABOUT THAT TIME

One date led to another and another. Some of them entailed barbecues at various friends' houses with more questionable guests. But as time went on, Yvette seemed to grow accustomed to the surroundings. However, she was never off guard. One day when she had made it home from a mid-day date with Geo, her phone rang.

"Hey, girl! Where the hell have you been? I haven't talked to you in a minute." It was Kelsey.

"I've been around," Yvette responded.

"I guess Geo has all your attention and all your time now. You went from skeptical and unsure to a M.I.A., Bonnie and Clyde type," she laughed. "What changed?"

"I just gave him the benefit of doubt and stopped being such a prude and being judgmental."

"Have you asked him the question yet?"

"What question?"

"You're so caught up now you forgot?" Kelsey laughed.

"No, I haven't. I'm going to ask."

"I guess you won't be going out with us tonight, which is why I was calling."

"You should have called me earlier. Geo and I are going to see a movie tonight."

"Wow, not another sideless barbecue?" Kelsey laughed hysterically. "What's the deal with that anyway?"

"I don't know," Yvette replied. He just told me that it's usually him and the guys and all they want is meat and drinks. Sides are not really a necessity for them unless the women want to make some. Otherwise, they just Q some meat, get a loaf of bread, eat, drink, smoke something and talk shit. "

"I guess. You be careful. You already said he's never at work, but he has all these extravagant things. You already know he must be a D boy."

"I'm going to find a way to bring it up tonight, because I need to know."

"Okay, girl bye. I will talk with you later."

As she got ready that night for her movie date with Geo, he called.

"Hey, I'm outside. Are you ready?"

Yvette had finally grew comfortable enough to let him pick her up at her home instead of meeting in their usual spot – the restaurant parking lot. She wasn't ready for him to meet her children. So she told him to call when he was outside.

"Yes, I will be out in a minute," Yvette said.

"Hey, Mom. There's a bad car parked outside and it's a candy red painted Mercedes-Benz," Jaden said as he came in from basketball practice. "Where are you going?"

"I'm going to the movies."

"With the dude in the car outside?"

"Mind your business! And don't question me. I'm grown and I'm the mom."

"That car looks like a D Boy car, Mama," Jaden smirked.

"Boy shut up. Go upstairs and take a shower. What the hell do you know about a D boy?" Yvette grabbed her purse and headed out the door. Geo got out of the car and opened the door for her smiling from ear-to-ear. He was fresh from the barbershop. Gucci shades were strapped to his face and his gold teeth gleamed. How could something she despised so much become so irrelevant? They soon arrived at The Movie Tavern where movie-goers could have dinner and drinks while watching a movie. About 30 minutes in, he noticed Yvette nodding off and about and hour and a half later, it was over.

"Great movie," Yvette said as they walked to his car.

"How would you know? You were falling asleep," Geo laughed.

"No I wasn't" Yvette said. "So where to now?"

"I figured we would go back to my brother's place and have a drink. He's out of town for the weekend."

"So where's your place? We're always going to your brother's place."

"I'm always in and out of town so I haven't gotten a place here. You know, our mother is back in Alabama. I go back and forth to check on her."

"That's wonderful. You're a good son," Yvette smiled.

"I would make an even better man to you." Geo laughed and Yvette blushed. The two pulled up to Ron's house and went inside. Geo turned on some music and poured wine for the both of them. They talked and laughed about life, old exes and whatever else they could think of. Yvette thought this would be a great time to ask if he was indeed a D-boy. But one thing she wanted to know even more than that was, why in the three months that they had been dating, he had never tried anything with her, not even as much as a kiss. Only hugs. She asked him and his reply was simple.

"I'm a gentleman, and I respect you. I also feel like we have plenty of time for sex."

After drinking throughout the night, Yvette wanted to see another side of Geo. Alcohol induced, her body screamed for more than a simple hug.

"What if I wanted you to be ungentleman-like for a change," Yvette said coyly. Usually, she was shy when it came to sexual initiation, but she was curious about this one. He hadn't made any sexual innuendos, no passes, no kisses, not even as much as a sexual conversation. *His penis must be small* she thought.

"You don't want that," he replied.

"Yes, yeah, I do." Yvette leaned in and kissed his soft full lips, pulling back a little to look up at him and catch his reaction. Then she leaned back in for more. Stunned at first by her forwardness, he relaxed and kissed her back. He put his hand on the back of her neck and pulled her closer and devoured her lips with his mouth passionately, as if he had been waiting on the go-ahead from her. The feel of his kisses set a fire inside of Yvette that she hadn't felt in a long time. She lost all self-control and pulled herself onto his lap and straddled him. Geo stopped kissing her for a second and asked, "Are you sure you are ready for this?"

"Look you're not going to keep coming around playing with my emotions. What's wrong? You have a girlfriend or something?"

"No, I don't have a girlfriend. I want to make sure you're ready and there are no regrets afterwards."

His eyes gleamed as he looked up at Yvette with concern and care.

"I'm ready and there will be no regrets. Yesss, I'm ready" she whispered seductively and placed her warm lips on his lips once again.

The kissing intensified, and at that point, she could feel his manhood rising higher and higher. Indeed he was not small. His apprehensiveness was not due to lack at all. She guessed he was trying to be a gentleman, and with the size of his endowment, he would need to be a gentleman tonight. Geo flipped her off of his lap and onto the couch. He climbed on top of her, lifted her shirt and kissed her ample breasts. His mouth was warm and wet on her breasts and it sent chills through every extremity of her body. Her heart raced. She had not been touched by a man since before her divorce. *Oh my God this is really about to happen* she thought. *I still don't know what this man does for a living.* He removed her panties. *What if he is a drug dealer? What if I get caught up in it?*

At the moment when hysteria and questions going on in her mind, he penetrated her and it felt like he entered her soul. She felt like someone had injected her with morphine. Every thought she had was replaced with extreme euphoria. She felt every inch of him, wall to wall and front to back. With every stroke, the sensation intensified and she went higher and higher with every thrust. Geo wasn't much of a talker during the act, but he sure knew how to handle his business. No words were needed. Yvette let out a moan of shear pleasure. She thought at one point her former husband was a triple threat in bed, but Geo was a truth, minus the oral portion, but that's okay. It was their first time. Maybe next time it will be included.

"Are you okay?" Geo asked.

"Yeah, I'm fine." Yvette tried to gather her composure.

"That was nice. Did you get yours?" Yvette asked. "I couldn't tell."

"Yeah, of course I did," Geo replied. "But you got me so turned on it won't stay down."

"That's a good thing," she smirked.

Over the next few months, Geo and Yvette grew closer and more sex ensued which made her fall for him even more. She was always a sucker for great sex.

Yvette finally introduced her children to him. They took a liking to him. The kids considered him laid-back and chilled. When Katrina's prom came up, he sent his Benz to a special detail shop that had it looking like it had just been driven off the showroom floor. The tires looked like they were dripping wet from rain, the rims shined like new diamonds, and the crimson candy red paint looked like it had diamond specs glistening in the sun. He parked it in front of the house and it was just for her and her friends.

"Oh, my God!" Katrina screamed. "I am going to be the envy of everyone at the prom."

Her friends were all excited as well. After photos were taken, Katrina and her friends loaded themselves into the car. Geo handed her the keys and said, "Enjoy yourself and be careful."

"Thank you, so much!" Katrina replied with a look of eternal gratitude in her eyes.

Geo and Yvette watched as she and her friends pulled off.

"Be home by 2!" Yvette yelled. Yvette and Geo went inside with plans of taking full advantage of not having the children home for the night. Jaden was away at basketball camp. They wanted a little adult time. Yvette poured two glasses of wine, lit some candles, and turned on music. The sultry sounds of neo-soul singer Kem played in the background. The name of the song was, "When Love Calls." It began to play. She looked at him like a lioness in heat. She wanted him to grab her and throw her on the floor and ravish her until she had third-degree carpet burns all over. The more she sipped, the more her craving intensified. The thought of him touching her made her body tingle in anticipation.

"You going to sit there like you don't want me, is that it?" Yvette asked lustfully.

Geo never came off like the aggressive type when it came down to sex, but once he got started, he turned into a beast that would have a woman begging for mercy. He chuckled and replied in a warm and sensuous tone.

"Come here," he commanded.

The flame flickered in his eyes from the candlelight.

"Hold on, wait one second," Yvette said as she retreated into the kitchen and came back with a bottle of chocolate syrup and a can of whipped cream.

She looked at him deviously. She set the two items down on the coffee table and said, "I'll be right back." When she returned she had two large beach towels in her hand and she wore the skin she was born in. Her long black hair draped over her breasts and made her look like Eve as she walked throughout the Garden of Eden. "This could get messy," she said seductively.

"Yes it could," Geo replied looking like he could easily feast on her all night.

Yvette laid both towels on the floor.

"Lay down," she ordered him. Geo did as he was told. She lifted his shirt over his head and made a trail of chocolate syrup and whipped cream from underneath his chin down his neck, the center of his chest, and stopped at his navel. Yvette laid down beside him and tilted his chin up. She slowly tasted every ounce of chocolate syrup from his body until there wasn't any more left. Geo gave off slight grunts of enjoyment, and tried to maintain his composure. She made her way to the area of his navel. She looked up him and said, "I saved the best for last." She unzipped his pants, reached in, and exposed his manhood which was cocked and loaded. She raised the chocolate syrup bottle and let it drip down slowly until it practically covered him.

Just as she was about to take him into her mouth, Geo asked, "What? No whip cream?"

Yvette replied, "I'm sure you'll have that covered in a minute." She winked at him and inhaled his penis into her warm wet mouth, and surrounded him with her soft lips.

Another night of incredible sex ensued. Yvette was growing attached to him and falling fast for Geo. As they lay there in a post sex haze, Yvette said, "There is something I've been meaning to ask you and I really want to know. Are you affiliated with any drugs whatsoever? Are you a drug dealer?"

Geo smiled and laughed a little.

"Why would you say that?"

"You don't work for from what I see. You always have money, you drive that nice-ass car, you constantly go out of town, so you say, to see your mom and take care of some business. But you never mention a job or what it is that you do."

"Look, we've been kicking it for a little while. I'm really feeling you, so I want to be honest with you. I hope you can handle it."

"Whatever it is, I need to know. I mean I'm feeling you, too. It's only fair that you tell me the truth."

"Okay." He took a deep breath. I do deal in a little business in that area, but I don't touch anything. I have people that make moves for me, therefore my hands are always clean."

Yvette swallowed hard. Although she suspected it, it was now confirmed. The sex haze left her almost instantly and was replaced with all types of thoughts, like Geo ending up in jail, her becoming that girlfriend who visits him twice a month, keeping money on his books, to being caught by the police with drugs in the car while they're out on a date.

"Oh, my God! The car!" she shouted. "You let my daughter use your car knowing you participate in this type of activity. I mean what if someone thinks she's you? What if some of the people you know see her in the car and approach her?" She immediately jumped to her feet and shouted. "Do you have drugs in your car?" Now she was nervous. "What if she gets stopped by the cops? I need to call her. I need to go to her prom and switch out the cars. Why would you do that?"

"Calm down!" Geo shouted. "You're doing the most, and overthinking things."

"Don't tell me I'm overthinking things. That's my child in your car, and you are a filthy drug dealer?"

"I'm filthy drug dealer huh? You didn't think that a few minutes ago. And don't act like you didn't have some idea. You said yourself you never heard me talk about a job, I'm in and out of town, I always have money and nice things. What, you needed to hear me say it?"

"Fuck you!" Yvette replied angrily.

"You just did that," Geo responded sarcastically. "So, you are just going to go up there and ruin her prom night trying to switch cars, right? How are you going to explain that to her and her friends, huh? This is supposed to be a great night that they will always remember and you're going to ruin it. I would never put you or those children in harm's way."

Yvette stood in the middle of the floor, wrapped in a beach towel with chocolate smeared on it. The candlelight bounced off her skin as she gazed to the side with a confused look. She certainly didn't want to ruin her daughter's prom night. Geo walked over to her and tried to reassure her. "Baby, she's going to be fine. She's probably safer in my car than she's ever been. Nobody will bother her. Trust me when I tell you she's good."

Yvette looked at Geo as if to say, "you better hope so," but instead she uttered the words, "I'm going to take a shower." She proceeded to the bathroom. The whole time she was in the shower, she prayed for Katrina's safe return home. Just before she got out, Geo came in the bathroom and got into the shower with her.

"You mind if I get some of this stickiness off me as well?" he asked.

"Sure, I was just getting out." Yvette stepped out of the shower, grabbed a towel, and went into the bedroom. Geo shook his head in disbelief because the evening had turned sour. Yvette got dressed and sat on the sofa anxiously waiting on her daughter to return. She looked at the clock every few minutes.

Geo sat in the chair across from her not wanting to say anything, but managed to say, "She's fine."

Yvette didn't hear anything. The noise in her head was so loud, she only had thoughts of Katrina.

At around 2:30 a.m., she heard a car door slam. She pulled back the curtains and it was Katrina and her friends. They had planned to finish out the rest of the prom as a sleepover. Katrina opened the door and saw that her mom and Geo were sitting there. She was shocked.

"Are you guys waiting up for me?" she asked with a sigh.

"No," Yvette replied with a smile of relief. "Geo was getting ready so he could leave when you guys got here." She then turned around and looked to the left where he was sitting. He looked back at her in defeat.

"We had an amazing time! Everybody was checking out your car. It really made my prom the best!" Katrina gushed with excitement.

"No problem. I'm glad you had fun," Geo responded. "Let me holla at you for a minute outside, Yvette."

They walked outside to his car. "What is your problem? You just going to shit on our entire night? She made it home safely like I told you. I would never put you or your children in harms' way." He tried his best to explain to her.

"I need some time to think," she replied.

"The next time you ask someone a question and they're 100 percent honest with you be prepared to accept it."

He got really close, within kissing distance of Yvette's face and said, "You knew who I was and what I was about deep down inside, but you were hoping and wanting me to be something else. I'm not. I'm me. He then walked away, got n his car, and sped off, leaving Yvette standing on the sidewalk with her arms folded. She was puzzled. *Maybe I hoped it wasn't the case. Perhaps I wanted to believe he was secretly, gainfully employed.*

CHAPTER 5
WHERE DO WE GO FROM HERE?

The next day, Yvette went to work as usual, with thoughts of Geo on her mind. He didn't call after he left her house as usual or even that morning. Lunch time came and went and there still wasn't a call.

It's probably for the best she thought. *I can't subject myself or my children to such a lifestyle.* Yvette didn't pick up the phone to call him, either.

She didn't know what to say to him. Instead, she called Elisha who had experience with guys in the game. Maybe she could give her some advice, after all, she really liked him in spite of their differences in lifestyle.

"Hey chick," Yvette said when Elisha answered.

"Oh, hey bitch! Now you want to call a sister. Geo finally let you come up for air?" Elisha scoffed.

"Girl, I'm sorry. I've been out of pocket for a minute."

"The sex must be all that. That's the only thing that will make a woman stop hanging with her girls and go MIA," Elisha laughed.

"I'm not going to lie; it was pretty amazing."

"Was? What do you mean was," Elisha questioned.

"I finally asked him and he admitted that he is indeed a drug dealer."

"Awwww, bitch. I could have told you that! What the hell did you think he did? I know your bougie ass couldn't possibly be that green," Elisha said.

"I guess part of me hoped it was not true," Yvette said.

"Well, keep hope alive as the Rev. says, but hope is not going to change the fact that he is a D boy."

"Maybe I can change that and show him a better way," Yvette said.

"There you go with that bullshit, wanting to change someone. Girl, what-you-see-is-what-you-get, work with it or leave it alone. If you know you're not about that life, let it go."

"I know, but I really like him," Yvette replied sadly."

"Bitch please, you like that pipe," Elisha laughed uncontrollably. "You better take your feelings out of this one and just enjoy the ride ... literally enjoy the ride."

"Anyways, how are you and the husband doing?"

"Girl, he is planning another all-guys' trip. I'm telling you, they either got some hoes that they are meeting up with every time they go on these trips, or their asses are gay. I mean what man constantly goes on trips with other guys and they all sleep in the same room where hoes aren't involved or some gay shit is not going on?"

"Have you said anything to him about it?"

"For what? It will come to the light. In the meantime, he can continue to do him and I will do me. As long as he keeps paying the bills in the house and he doesn't get sloppy with it, I'm good."

"I don't see how you do it. I couldn't deal with it knowing that there's a possibility my husband is cheating."

"They all cheat. Find me one that won't. You got to play the game how it goes. Your ass is always catching feelings. You better keep your game face locked and loaded if you plan to run with these Texas boys. You are not in Cali anymore, chick."

"Whatever," Yvette laughed. "I got to get back to work. I will talk to you later."

"Okay, girl. Remember keep your game face on."

"Okay, bye, girl."

Once Yvette got home, she started dinner. She still hadn't heard anything from Geo, nor had she bothered to call him. She opened up the fridge to get out some veggies to cook and saw the bottle of chocolate syrup and can of whipped cream from the last night they spent together. She immediately began to reminisce: the smell of his cologne, the softness of his lips kissing her body in all the right places. The thrusting of his body against hers, how mellow and mild-tempered he always was no matter what.

"Mom, why are you standing here with the refrigerator door open?" Jaden asked as he came downstairs into the kitchen for a snack. He had found Yvette standing there with the refrigerator door open, in deep thought.

"Oh, I forgot what I was looking for," Yvette said as she snapped out of her Geo-driven trance.

"You look like you were in deep thought," Jaden replied.

"Boy get your snack and go back upstairs. What do you know about someone being in deep thought?"

Jaden grabbed his chips and juice and went back upstairs. *I should give him a call* she thought. She picked up the phone and dialed his number. He answered on the first ring.

"Hey, how are you?" Yvette asked.

"I'm good," Geo replied. "And you?"

"I'm good, too. I hadn't heard from you since the other night."

"You seemed like you were mad about my truth and who I am. I wanted to give you your space to decide if you want to continue to deal or not deal with me."

"Look," Yvette said. "I really like you. I like you a lot. I think our chemistry is amazing and I can't stop thinking about you."

"I can't stop thinking about you, either," Geo replied.

"Man, do you know how hard it was for me not to pick up the phone and call you? I knew you were upset and I wanted to give you some time. Look, Yvette, I know my lifestyle is different from yours, and we probably grew up on different sides of the track, but this is how me and my family eat and how I help my friends and their family eat. I afford myself and my family a lifestyle that a regular nine-to-five can't. I take care of my mom and all her bills, my son, my sisters, and my nieces. I've been doing this for so long I can't let them down, and I would do the same for you and yours. I promise you I would never let anything happen to you or those kids."

This was definitely not the man, Yvette had planned to fall in love with, and at this point she wasn't sure if it was love but she knew it was something really deep. She couldn't shake the feelings she had for him. She thought about what Elisha said, "just enjoy the ride."

"I'm not going to lie to you, your lifestyle does scare me, but I can't deny our connection. So when am I going to see you again? And I'm not taking no for an answer."

"I'm in the process of cooking right now. Why don't you come by for dinner later?"

"Sounds good to me. Do you want me to bring anything?"

"Why don't you bring a bottle of Chardonnay?"

"Oh, you're a wine drinker," he teased.

"Yes, I am. So, I'll see you around 7:30."

"Yeah, I will see you then. I can't wait to see your face. I miss you."

"I miss you, too."

Later that night, Yvette prepared dinner. She had Jaden and Katrina to eat earlier, that way she and Geo could have some alone time downstairs.

"Dinner was good. So you can cook?" Geo laughed.

"You didn't think I could cook?" Yvette smiled with her hands on her hips.

"Most pretty girls can't cook well," he said and grabbed her around her waist, and kissed her fully on the lips. Yvette's entire body got hot in a flash.

"Whew! That's enough of that Chardonnay," she said and took a deep breath. I am so aroused right now."

"In that case, keep drinking," Geo said. He spun her around so that her back faced him. He moved her hair to the side and softly kissed the back of her neck. He lifted her shirt up and ran his tongue down her spine.

Yvette turned around. "We can't. The kids are here.

"Then don't scream like last time," he said with a mischievous grin.

He then pulled her towards the bedroom. Thank God Yvette's room was downstairs. No doubt the kids would have heard something had it not been. Yvette didn't know why but it was something about Chardonnay that took her sex game to a whole nother level. She almost became someone else. Her hormones peaked 1,000 times over the norm and there were no limitations. She could go all night having orgasm after orgasm. They switched positions with the sheets soaking wet from sweat and the sexual juices. The night seemed to never end, and Yvette didn't care. Passion and pleasure ensued until they both fell asleep.

Just before daybreak, Yvette awakened. She nudged Geo and said, "You got to go. Get up. I'm not ready for the kids to wake up and see you here."

Geo was understanding. He reached down, picked up his clothing from the floor and got dressed. Yvette walked him to the door. He turned around and kissed her. "I enjoyed you. When am I going to see you again?"

"When do you want to?" Yvette asked.

"Today, tomorrow, and every day after that," he replied.

"I will see what I can do," she smiled, then kissed him.

"Make that happen," he said, then walked to his car and drove away.

Over the course of a couple of years, Geo and Yvette broke up and got back together. Yvette had a hard time here and there accepting Geo's lifestyle. No matter how much she cared for him, she was always on high alert everywhere they went. He assured her that he never carried anything on him and would never put her in a bad position, but that never stopped her from thinking the worst. Yvette became comfortable enough to allow him to spend nights and even stay until morning, allowing her children to actually see them together when they awakened.

The words, "I love you" were exchanged. Geo even tried to change his lifestyle and get a legitimate job to put Yvette's mind at ease. This made her happy. She was no longer afraid. Geo, on the other hand, had a hard time dealing with the change. He went from fast money to waiting on a paycheck every week. That situation wouldn't last long for him, but he loved her enough to try. He knew it was a matter of time before something had to give. He loved her but he also love the streets and the lifestyle it provided him. It was all he had ever known.

"Hey baby, I need to go out of town this weekend and see my mom. I want you to go with me and meet her and my sisters. Why don't you take off for the weekend?"

"Wow, you want me to meet your mom? It's official now," she laughed.

"I talk about you all the time. She knows who you are. She knows about all the times we broke up and got back together. She knows about all of that. In fact she was the one who kept telling me that if I truly care about you, don't give up."

"I'd be happy to meet your mom," Yvette said with excitement.

CHAPTER 6
THE RIDE

The weekend came and Yvette was officially ready to meet Geo's family. "Are we going to do anything special?" she asked. "I need to know so I can pack accordingly."

"Don't do all that extra stuff, with heels and all. My family is pretty low-key. We will probably barbecue and hang out in the yard, nothing special," Geo said. He loaded a couple of duffel bags in the car.

"You don't want to put these in the trunk?" she asked.

"No, I have those speakers in there. There's not really any room in the trunk."

Yvette opened the passenger door and was about to get in when Geo asked, "Babe, you think you can drive for a little while? I was out with the guys late last night and I didn't get any sleep. It's a six-hour drive. I figured I would get a nap in right quick then swap the last three hours. You know, you do half and I do the other?"

She had not anticipated driving. She had hoped to be sitting pretty in the passenger seat the whole way, but this was her man and she wanted to take care of him like he did for her.

"No problem, babe," she responded and got out of the passenger seat and into the driver's seat. Yvette started the car and they were on their way to Alabama. They talked and laughed and listened to music for about an hour. After that, Geo was knocked out sleep. Yvette turned the music up slightly and continued to drive. She got caught up in the music and drove well over her agreed three hours. Geo had taken one hell of a nap.

"Hey babe, we are almost there," she said as she nudged him awake. I don't know where to go from here.

"Damn, I must have really been tired. Pull over at this gas station. Let's use the restroom, get more gas, and I will take it from here."

"Really!" Yvette laughed.

"You only have an hour to drive before we make it to your mom's house. It's okay though. You were resting so peacefully I didn't want to wake you."

"Thanks, babe, I appreciate that." Geo smiled and kissed Yvette on the lips in a show of gratitude. He refueled the car while she went inside to use the restroom.

On the way back, Yvette picked up a few snacks and a few bottles of water for the road. The two met at the counter to pay for the items and began the last hour-long drive on to Alabama.

"Hey, babe we are here," Geo said.

Yvette had fallen asleep.

"I guess I was tired, too," she said as she wiped her eyes and checked her makeup in the visor mirror.

"You ready?" Geo asked.

"I'm ready. Let's do this."

Geo's mother's house was quite modest. It was a far cry from the houses in the area of Dallas where Yvette lived. Geo rang the doorbell and a little dark-skinned lady with glasses wearing a Jerri curl opened the door.

"Hey, Tony, you made it! So glad to see you, baby!" Yvette was taken off guard. *Tony?*

"You must be Yvette," the lady said.

"Yes, ma'am," Yvette replied.

"Nice to meet you, I'm Laura May. Come on in and make yourself at home. I'm cooking a little something for later. Are y'all hungry?" she asked.

"We had a few snacks on the way so we are not starving, but we could eat something," Geo said as he rummaged through his mom's fridge.

"Boy, get out of my refrigerator! Have you washed your hands? You just came off the road and you're in my fridge you know I don't play that."

"Mom, my hands are clean!"

"Tony get out of my refrigerator and go wash up now!" his mom yelled.

"Okay, Ma," Geo laughed.

"The room is all ready for y'all. There are towels in the cabinet if you want to shower."

"Thank you, Miss Laura, Yvette said with a warm smile."

"You're welcome dear," she replied.

The pair retreated into the room and unpacked fresh clothes in order to shower and freshen up. Geo went into the bathroom that was connected to the bedroom and turned the shower on.

"You ready, babe?" he asked.

Yvette answered as he undressed to get into the shower. "Ready for what?" she asked.

"To get in the shower," he responded.

"Boy, I'm not taking a shower with you at your mom's house!"

"Why not?" Geo asked.

"That's disrespectful. I will wait until you get out."

"Girl if you don't come and get in the shower ... My mom may be older and she may be my mom, but she's not old fashioned. She's real."

"I don't feel comfortable with that, Geo," Yvette said, clearly concerned.

"Look, you either take your clothes off and come get in the shower or ..." he stopped and walked up to her and pressed his naked body against hers. He whispered seductively in her ear. "I'm going to take them off for you." A warm sensation shot through Yvette's body. "I kind of like the thought of that," she responded.

Slowly Geo removed Yvette's clothing piece by piece then grabbed her hand and lead her into the shower. The two of them took turns lathering each other's body. The steam from the hot shower filled the air, clouded the mirrors and shower doors. Geo lathered the towel and slowly washed Yvette's neck, circled her breasts and trailed down her stomach. He slowly and gently cupped her flower and began slowly stroking.

"Don't do that," Yvette whispered.

"Ssshhh," Geo whispered back.

Oh, my God Yvette thought. *I can't believe this.* At the same time she did not want it to stop.

He slowly kissed her on her neck, then circled her nipples with his tongue. In the same fashion, he kissed her stomach, and fell to his knees in the shower, as he cupped her firm ass in his hands.

Yvette knew this was not going to end well. It would but it wasn't a good idea to do it here, at his mom's house. After all, it was Yvette's first time meeting her. *This is not right* she thought to herself.

"Baby, please, don't do this. Your mom is in the other room. Please stop!"

Yvette grabbed his head in an attempt to push him away. He removed her hand and looked up at her with the shower water running all over his face and whispered, "relax." And with that one word he plunged his tongue inside her, moving the petals of her feminine flower aside until he came to the center then vigorously back and forth he delighted her with his mouth, and pleasured her right there.

With every flick of his tongue, Yvette found it hard to control her emotions. She grabbed him by the back of his head as he consumed her. He moved his head from side to side and up and down. Yvette thought she would pass out from trying to hold in her moans. She grabbed a towel that hung from the shower rod in an effort to muffle her moans. Finally, her body tensed up and a sweet release followed. Yvette's body weakened.

Geo stood up, looked at her, and said, "I told you to relax."

He kissed her on the cheek and got out of the shower. Once Yvette regained her composure, she shut off the water and got out of the shower.

"How am I going to look at your mom now knowing what just happened?" she asked.

"Did you enjoy it?" he asked with a smirk.

"Yes, but that's not the point. I am embarrassed." She put the towel over her face.

"Stop it," he laughed. "It's not that serious. Don't go out there looking guilty."

The two of them dried off, got dressed and went into the living area where his mom watched TV.

"Dinner is ready. Y'all want to eat?" Miss Laura asked.

"Yeah, I'm ready to eat," Geo responded. "But not too much, Mom. I know how you like to make gigantic plates of food. I had a little snack cake earlier," he said and winked at Yvette. "It kind of took the edge off my hunger."

Yvette's eyes grew big with embarrassment.

"What kind of snack cake was that," his mom asked. "Was it one of those little Debbie snack cakes?"

"As a matter of fact it was," Geo said. He smiled because he knew Yvette's mom's name was Debbie.

"Which one? You know I love those Little Debbie snack cakes."

"Me too." Geo looked at Yvette and smiled broadly.

"It was the chocolate one with the creamy white filling."

"Oh, those are really good, his mom exclaimed.

"I know, right?" Geo said. "Really good!"

Yvette thought she would die from guilt. After dinner it was late so they said their goodnights and retreated into the bedroom to sleep. Laying in bed thinking about the day and all that transpired, Yvette had one burning question. "Hey, babe are you awake?"

"What's up?" Geo asked. "Yes I am awake."

"Why does your mother call you Tony, but I know you as Geo?" she asked.

"My government name is Antonio Giovanni Jameson, but in the streets they call me Geo for short from my middle name. I grew up being called Tony by my family because my first name is Antonio."

"Oh, okay, then I should call you Tony."

"No, you keep calling me what you've been calling me. Besides. I never liked my first name anyway." Geo's phone rang. "Yeah, man I'm in town. I'm laying down with my baby about to go to sleep. Oh? I haven't seen him in a minute. Okay, I will come around there for a minute." Geo hung up the phone.

"Babe I'm going to go meet up with a few of the fellas for a minute. My high school friend is in town that I haven't seen in years."

"Really? Geo, it's midnight. Where y'all going to hang out at this time of night?" Yvette questioned.

"I'm only going a few streets over and meet up with them at his house for a couple of hours. I will be back. Get you some sleep. I know you're tired."

Yvette was not happy about being left alone at the house on the first night she met his mom, but at this point she thought she would go ahead and get some rest. Geo left around 12:30 a.m. despite what Yvette felt. She eventually fell asleep. A few hours went by. She woke up to use the bathroom and noticed that Geo was not home. She check the time on her phone and it was 4 a.m. Yvette called him but didn't get an answer. Soon as she hung up, he called back. "Where the hell are you?" she asked.

"I'm still hanging out with the fellas, babe, and handling a little business," he responded.

"What do you mean? It's four in the morning! What kind of business? You sound like you've been drinking."

"I'll be there in a minute. Let me take care of this and let me let my boys know I'm leaving."

"Take care of what?" Yvette said angrily. "You brought me all the way here to leave me with your mom while you go hang out!"

"I will be on my way in a minute." Geo hung the phone up abruptly before Yvette could say another word. This only infuriated her.

Thirty minutes passed by, then an hour but still no Geo. Yvette called his phone but he didn't answer. As the darkness turned into daylight, Geo finally made it back to his mom's house at 6:15 a.m. By this time, Yvette was red-hot mad.

"Babe, I'm so sorry. I had too much to drink and passed out at my boy's house." Yvette didn't respond. "Would you rather me drive back and risk getting into an accident or getting a DUI?"

Yvette still said nothing. She lay on her side with her back towards him. She knew if she said one word to him in that state of mind it would not go over well.

Later, around 10 a.m., they got dressed and met his mom in the kitchen for breakfast. Still visibly upset and not speaking to Geo, Yvette walked into the kitchen.

"Good morning, Miss Laura," she said.

"Good morning, dear, did you sleep well?" she asked.

"I slept okay," Yvette responded.

"Just okay?" Miss Laura was fishing. She sensed a bit of tension between the two. Geo explained. "She's a bit pissed off at me. I went and met up with Daryl and the guys and had a few drinks. I got a little drunk and stayed until I sobered up."

"I will be mad at you, too," his mom said. "First off, you should know how to control yourself. Secondly, I heard you come in at 6 a.m. That's wrong of you to do that to her. Did you bring her here to sit around while you hang out?"

"No, it's just the guys called ... I didn't plan to be out that late. We got to talking about old times and time got away from me. I'm sorry, Yvette."

Yvette still didn't say anything.

"Yvette you can't stay mad, sugar. You got to let it go. He has apologized," Miss Laura said.

"Fine, I accept your apology," Yvette said grudgingly.

"Okay, now let's eat this breakfast," his mom said.

Geo went over to her and gave her a kiss and they ate breakfast. Later that day, Yvette and Geo got invited to his sister's house for a barbecue and a game of spades. It was also an opportunity for the rest of the family to meet Yvette. They drove over and Geo got out of the car and opened the door for Yvette.

"You look nice, babe. My sisters are going to love you."

"Thanks," Yvette said. She was still a little upset about Geo's early morning arrival. They walked up to the house and without knocking, Geo opened the door and walked right in. People were inside and outside in the backyard.

"Boy, don't just walk in my house like that," a lady said as she peeked around the corner from the kitchen.

"You need to keep the door locked," Geo said. "Yvette, this is my oldest sister, Pam, and this is her husband, Terry."

"Nice to meet you," Yvette said.

"Welcome. Have a seat. We are about to get us a spade game going. Do you play?" Pam asked.

"No, I don't too much care for card games," Yvette replied.

"What?" Pam said. "No spades?

You must not be from the south."

"No, I'm from the West Coast. I have family members who play. I just don't care to," she explained.

Throughout the day more introductions were exchanged. Yvette met the two other sisters, nieces, nephews, cousins and friends. The barbecue was delicious and they actually had side dishes to go with the barbecue. Drinks flowed, music played, and spade games went on and on. Yvette finally let go of her disappointment and anger. She relaxed and enjoyed the family atmosphere. She sat next to Geo while he played cards and rubbed his back as if to say, "I forgive you." He looked up at her and grinned, followed by a wink.

"Come and sit with us on the porch, Yvette," Pam said. Yvette got up to walk to the front door. Geo grabbed her hand and pulled her toward him and kissed her before she walked out.

"Oh, my goodness," Pam said.

"We're not going to eat her up."

"Please, don't," Geo said. "Leave that up to me."

He smacked Yvette on her behind as she passed by him. Once on the porch, Yvette grabbed the chair and sat down with his three sisters, Andrea, Denise, and Pam. They sat, talked, and asked questions like sisters do. More drinks were followed by more music. Everything felt great. Pam opened up about her past lifestyle of flipping money by selling drugs out of her home with her brother Geo when he was younger. Yvette couldn't believe her ears. *I guess alcohol is truth serum* she thought. Geo came out of the house with one of his friends.

"Babe, we are about to run to the store and get some more alcohol."

"Okay, don't be gone all day long," Yvette said.

"We are going in his car so you know I'm not going to be gone too long. Here are the keys to my car, in case you need them."

He gave Yvette a kiss and proceeded to get in the car with his friend and drive off. At that moment, Yvette felt an unsettling feeling in her stomach as she watched Geo ride off.

"Come on and have a seat. He'll be right back. We ain't going to bite you girl," Pam said.

Yvette managed to smile and sit down. She laughed and talked with the sisters. Time went by and eventually, Yvette realized Geo had been gone for two hours. Yvette got worried. She walked over to Geo's car and gave him a call.

Geo answered, "Hey, babe, what's up?"

"What do you mean what's up?" Yvette replied angrily. "Where the hell are you? I didn't come here to spend time with your family without you. You brought me all the way here. This is the second time you have left me alone with your family."

"What kind of shit is this? Babe, I had to take care of something. I will be back in a minute."

"You told me you were going to the store and that was over two hours ago. You need to get here now!" Yvette shouted.

"I gotta handle this. I'll be there when I get there!" Geo shouted and hung up the phone on Yvette.

I know the hell he did not hang up on me, she thought. She attempted to call Geo back several times but he wouldn't answer. This infuriated Yvette. A couple more hours went by. It started to rain but still no Geo.

Yvette felt lost and alone. She was stranded in a place where she knew no one. She had just met these people. *How could he do this?*

Yvette walked back to the car again to call once more but to no avail. Her anger soon turned to tears. She was that mad. Yvette called Elisha to vent.

"Hey girl, what's up?" Elisha answered.

"Girl, you won't believe. I have gotten all the way here and this motherfucker has left me by myself with his family twice for four hours," Yvette sobbed.

"Oh, hell no! What? Why? What is his reason for that?" Elisha asked.

"He keeps talking about he has some business to take care of," Yvette quivered between crying.

"Business? Business?" Elisha said.

"His ass out there hustling, girl. That's what the hell he's doing."

"Why would he bring me this far and do that while I'm here?" Yvette said.

"Honey, please, I told you to keep your game face on didn't I? Now you over there crying and all that shit."

"Girl, he just pulled up. Let me call you back," Yvette said.

"If you need me, call me back. I will get you a ticket so you can come back home. You don't need his ass," Elisha said.

"Okay, I will keep you posted." Yvette let the visor down, wiped her tears and fixed her make up. While doing so she heard a tap on the car window.

"What are you doing sitting out here in the car?" he asked.

Yvette looked up at him and if looks could kill, he would be DOA at the local hospital. He walked around to the passenger side and got into the car.

"I asked you why you are sitting out here? You are just going to ignore me?"

"After sitting and trying to get to know your family in your absence I pretty much ran out of things to talk about," she glared at him angrily.

"Man, I had to come out here and finish up some business. I can't just leave the game like that, but I tried and I did it for you! If I don't make these moves my people can't eat."

"So you brought me all the way out here to do that!" Yvette yelled. "You could have left me at home."

"You're always hollering about I'm always gone, so I brought you with me. I don't know what the hell for!"

"It was the same as being home but worse. I don't know your family and you dump me off and run the streets!"

"I'm not running the streets!" Geo slammed his fist on the dashboard of the car. I'm out here taking penitentiary chances for my family, for us. I'm not a nine-to-five man Yvette! I'm a hustler, I'm from the streets. This is all I know and what I'm good at doing."

"Why didn't you leave me at home," she yelled.

"I don't want to be a part of this."

"I wanted you to meet my family, and I needed you," he paused.

"Needed me for what?" Yvette asked.

"I found out my driver's license was suspended and I had to get here. My head was on the chopping block for some unfinished business here. A lot of things were riding on me making it out here to finish some business I started."

"So you fucking used me? It wasn't about me meeting your folks. You needed someone with a valid license to drive you!"

"Babe, I wanted you to meet my mother and I had to handle that as well," he stated.

"Did you have drugs in the car on the way here?" Yvette questioned him. Geo just stared off to the side. Yvette yelled louder, "Did you have drugs in the car?" Then she stopped and thought for a second. "You did, you did. That's why you didn't put the bags in the trunk of the car."

"Me stopping all of a sudden like that put me in a huge bind, but I did it. I tried to be that man for you.

I had some unfinished business that I had to handle or else."

"Take me home!" Yvette yelled. "Take me home! You said you would never put me at risk like that and you did. I can't trust you. Take me home!"

"Take you home? I'm here trying to make moves for us. That house you said you wanted, the new car, the purses. I can't get that for you working a job paying $17 an hour. I'm doing this for us and you want me to take you home? You will go home when I'm done, otherwise find your own way home!" Geo snatched his keys get out of the car and went into his sister's house.

Yvette was in disbelief and began to sob uncontrollably. She could not believe she had gotten herself into this predicament. She called Elisha, who heard her sobbing and without a word from Yvette, she said, "I'm already looking up flights. Can you be at the airport in the next couple of hours?"

"Yes, Yvette said softly through her tears. I'm going to call a cab now." About 20 minutes later, a Yellow Cab pulled up and Yvette emerged from Geo's car where she had been sitting since their fiery exchange. The family saw the cab and immediately informed Geo. He rushed out of the house.

"So, you are going to leave like that?" he asked. Pam followed him out.

"Don't leave like this. Can't you two talk about this?" she asked.

Yvette looked at her with red and puffy eyes and said, "There's no more to talk about."

"So, you're going to leave? What about your clothes at Mama's house?" Geo asked.

"Burn them to ashes just like you did this relationship." And with that statement, Yvette got into the cab and proceeded to the airport. She never looked back.

CHAPTER 7
IT'S NOT OVER

The next day while at work, Yvette's phone lit up like a Christmas tree. She didn't answer it. She knew it was Geo. He had been calling her ever since she pulled off in the cab. Yvette never answered. The work day went on and before she knew it, it was time to go home. On the drive home, she thought about Geo. She really loved him and cared for him, but she felt used.

How could he put her in that position? What if they have been pulled over by the cops? What if some rivals knew he had drugs in the car and wanted to rob him? Yvette ran through so many what ifs in her head and she could not bear the thought of trusting him with her life or being around her children. She pulled into the driveway. She was exhausted. She opened the door and went to her bedroom to shower.

When she opened her bedroom door, she was met with a surprise. Hanging from her ceiling fan were several garments. Two were dresses and others were blouses. Laying on the bed were two purses, one Gucci, the other Chanel, with matching wallets. On the floor were two pair of shoes; Giuseppe's and Jimmy Choos.

As Yvette looked at the items she heard a voice from behind her ask, "Do you like them?"

Startled, she dropped the shoes, and turned around. It was Geo. "How in the hell did you get in here?" she asked.

"Jayden let me in. I was getting ready to knock and he was on his way to basketball practice. I told him I wanted to leave you some gifts and he let me in and went on to practice. I told him I would lock the door."

"He should not have done that. I will talk to him when he gets home."

"Talk to him for what? He knows me. I'm not a stranger, Yvette. I have spent nights here. We have done things like a family. Don't act like that," Geo pleaded.

"Not anymore. I can't trust you. I don't want you and that lifestyle around me or my children."

Geo rebutted loudly. "That lifestyle is how I take care of my family. That lifestyle is what bought these things that you see here. Isn't this the kind of stuff you said you wanted along with the big house? A nine-to-five isn't going to do it. I didn't finish college, and I'm not a rapper but I majored in the streets. Hustlin' is my talent and I'm good at it."

"I don't want any of it!" Yvette screamed. "Not like this." She snatched the garments from the ceiling fan and shoved them into Geo's arms and said, "Please take the stuff and go!"

"Just like that, huh? he asked. Yvette turned her back and sobbed. Geo pulled a gun from his waistband and fired a shot through the floor.

Yvette turned around. She was startled and scared. He walked towards her and put the gun to her head. Yvette felt the warm barrel against her temple and immediately began to silently pray.

"I tried to change for you. You gave me no credit. I'm not that dude, Yvette. I'm a hustler," Geo yelled. "I tried and it's not me!" Yvette never opened her eyes to look at him. She continued to pray harder. She never thought in a million years that it would come to this. "I love, you, Yvette. I was doing it for us. I don't know any other way. Open your eyes and look at me!" he demanded.

She opened her eyes and looked at him. The fear that he saw in her eyes was more hurtful to him than anything in the world. Geo saw the tears streaming down her face, and when he looked at her eyes, it was like she had seen the devil. It hurt him to see her look at him that way.

"What am I doing?" he said. "I could never hurt you. I love you. All I wanted was for you to accept me as I am. Why Yvette? Why couldn't you?" He took the gun away from Yvette's head and said, "I'll just kill myself since you don't want me. The only lifestyle I know may cause me to end up dead anyway. There's no way out of it but death or jail and I will never go there." He left out of the door, gun in hand. He turned around, looked coldly at Yvette and said, "You better not call the police or it will just be a shootout between me and them. You did this. Remember that." He closed the door behind him.

Yvette let out a big gasp of relief but her body still trembled with fear. She ran to lock the front door and picked up the phone to call the police, but she remembered what he said. Even though he had put a gun to her head she didn't want him to be killed, nor did she want her children and neighbors to be involved with this type of drama. She looked out the window and saw him sitting in the car. He had not started it. The windows were rolled up. *Oh, my God. He's going to kill himself in front of the house. What am I going to do?*

She thought to call his brother Ron. He lived about 10 minutes away. Maybe he could talk some sense into him. Yvette nervously dialed Ron's number. A husky voice answered.

"Hello, Ron," she whispered. "I need you to come to my house as fast as you can please! Your brother is here and he has a gun."

"What?" Ron shouted. What in the hell is going on? I'm on my way." Yvette nervously watched from the window wondering what was going on inside the car still parked in front of the house. She couldn't see inside because of the dark-tinted windows. Minutes went by but seemed like hours as she waited for Ron to get there.

A black Dodge Ram truck pulled up fast and came to a screeching halt. The doors of the truck flung open on both sides and out came Ron, Pam, and Miss Laura, who happened to be in town visiting relatives. Yvette opened the door and yelled, "He's sitting in the car! He put a gun to my head and then got in his car threatening to kill himself!"

Geo's family went to his car and tried to open the doors. When that failed, they tapped on the windows. He unlocked the door and emerged from the vehicle.

"You called my family?" he shouted angrily at Yvette.

"I didn't know what else to do. I didn't want to see you hurt yourself."

"Why? You don't give a fuck? I gave you all of me. I tried to change but nothing was ever good enough! You knew who I was and what I was about when you met me! Why couldn't you just accept me for who I was? I loved you. I just wanted to take care of you and the children and this is how you do me?"

"Man, what the hell is wrong with you?" Ron yelled.

"You over here with guns and shit. You want to go to jail? The pussy ain't worth all of that! Man, get your ass in your car. Let's go, before the neighbors call the cops."

"Yeah, come on, go get in the car," Pam said. "She's not worth all this." She gave Yvette the side eye.

Geo listened to his sister and brother and got in his car, but before he did, he had one more thing to say to Yvette.

"You will see me again," he smirked. Yvette didn't know how to take that. Was it a threat? She wasn't sure. She stood on the steps in disbelief at everything that had just happened. Before leaving with her children, Miss Laura walked up the steps to where Yvette was standing and held Yvette's hand.

"You call me, you hear me? This is not the man I raised. He's hurt right now and just because things are not great between the two of you doesn't mean you have to stop talking to me, okay?"

Yvette began to sob. "Pam and Ron seem to be mad at me and I did nothing. I could have called the cops, but I didn't do that. Your son put a gun to my head and I still thought of him and didn't call the cops. She sobbed louder. I loved him, Miss Laura. I just can't live that life. I thought out of my love for him I could, but I can't."

"They are siblings, Miss Laura said. "Naturally, they are going to take up for one another, but I'm off of what's right and what he did here today was wrong. It could have gone really bad. So as a mother, his mother, I thank you for choosing to call his family." The sound of a horn blew loudly. It was Ron.

"Come on, Mom let's go!" he shouted.

Miss Laura turned to walk to the truck where Pam and Ron waited, but before she completely walked away, she turned back, looked at Yvette and said, "I know you love my son, but you do what's best for Yvette, first. Remember that." Yvette watched Geo's mom walk away and ride off with Ron. Geo followed behind them. As he drove off, he rolled down his window and gave Yvette one last look, but this wasn't his normal look. Yvette didn't know what to make of it. She turned away and went inside and sobbed until she fell asleep. Yvette never did call or talk to Geo's mom again after that day in spite of her urging. She thought it was best that way. In spite of how close they had grown during her relationship with him, Yvette wanted to get back into her normal routine of work and family.

Yet, she could not get that day out of her head. She was tormented by the feel of the hot gun barrel against her temple, the look of anger mixed with hurt in Geo's eyes, along with the stare he gave her as he drove away.

She didn't know what to think, or what to expect from day to day. Was he angry enough to come after her? What exactly did he mean when he said you will see me again? All sorts of things began to play out in Yvette's mind. She decided to get some protection ... just in case. *I have to get a gun and protect myself.*

CHAPTER 8
GETTING LIFE BACK IN ORDER

Later in the week, Yvette called Elisha. "Hey, girl, I was thinking, why don't you, me, and Kelsey go to the gun range and learn how to shoot guns?" Yvette asked.

"Bitch what?" Elisha asked. "What brought this on? Who in the hell are you trying to kill?"

"Nobody," Yvette said. "I think it's a good idea that we as women know how to protect ourselves."

"Oh hell, what happened?" Elisha asked.

"Nothing girl," Yvette insisted.

"Yeah okay," Elisha replied, not completely convinced. "When do you want to do this?"

"Let's find a day this week that works for all three of us. There's a place not too far from me that I pass every day on my way to work."

Yvette never shared with anyone what happened that day with Geo, especially the fact that he pulled a gun on her.

A few days later, Elisha, Kelsey, and Yvette met up at the gun range. The instructor came out and introduced himself.

"Hi, ladies my name is Mitchell, and today's class is approximately four hours long. You will learn gun safety, how to properly handle your weapon, and how to shoot. Once that is done, you will walk away with a certification of completion in which you will be able to apply for your concealed handgun carrier's license.

"Four hours," Kelsey complained. "I have things to do. Yvette you didn't say it was going to be four hours."

"Girl, what do you have to do? Run behind that married Jamaican Rasta that's not going to leave his wife?" Elisha laughed.

"Don't try me," Kelsey said to Elisha. That's not funny."

"Ladies come on. It's going to go by fast and it's worth it. We will be pistol-toting sisters," Yvette excitedly said.

"Whatever," Kelsey said. "Let's get this over with."

"The instructor is kind of hot," Elisha said lustfully.

Mitchell was a brown-skinned brother, extremely fit with bulging muscles, sporting a tapered haircut, with neatly-trimmed goatee. He wore a pair of Versace prescription glasses, and stood about five-foot five. He looked intellectual.

"There you go, Yvette," Elisha said.

"Now that's your type of man right there."

"Girl, he's too short," Yvette responded.

"Bitch you're short!" Elisha expressed.

"Just because I'm short, doesn't mean I want a short man. I like my men tall, at least taller than me when I put my heels on."

"Yeah, you and every woman in the world and you see where that got you."

The class began. While Mitchell instructed the class, Yvette thought to herself, *he is quite handsome, why couldn't he be at least 6 ft tall?* She gave him a once-over then again once more, *yeah not bad* she thought, *but not for me.* Class continued and the trio tried out a couple of guns they felt comfortable with, under Mitchell's instruction. The four hours went by fast and soon the class was over. The ladies were certified and ready to get their concealed handgun carrier's license.

"Yay, we are done," Yvette said with excitement.

"Yeah, yeah, whatever. I still feel like it's something you're not telling me. Why all of a sudden an interest in a concealed handgun license?" Kelsey asked.

"Let's go catch a happy hour or something," Elisha suggested.

The ladies gathered their belongings and headed out of the door, but not before Mitchell and Yvette locked eyes on the way out.

A few months went by and Yvette's life seem to be getting back to normal. There were times when her thoughts would take her back to the wonderful times and intimate times she and Geo shared. She often felt lonely but felt no other man would measure up to the way she felt for him. The phone rang.

"Hi, is this Yvette?" a man's voice asked.

"Yes, this is she," Yvette responded.

"Hi, there. This is Mitchell from the gun range."

"Oh, hi Mitchell. How are you?"

"Great, hey listen. There was an error in your address so I wasn't able to send your certification. I was calling to get a correction on the address or to see if you wanted to stop by and pick it up."

"You're on my way home, so I will just stop by," Yvette said. "And you can save a stamp."

"Sounds good to me," Mitchell replied. "See you then."

After work, Yvette stopped by. "Hi, I'm here to pick up my certification from Mitchell," Yvette said to the woman at the front desk.

At that moment Mitchell walked out of a class.

"Hey, Yvette, give me one second. I'll be right back. Let me go to my office and get that for you."

Once again, Yvette took notice of Mitchell's physique. He had nicely tone muscles in all the right places.

It wasn't too much but just enough and definitely noticeable. She could tell that he was into fitness.

"Here you go. Now you're official," Mitchell said with a smile.

"Thank you," Yvette said. "You were an awesome instructor."

"Thank you, I do my best," Mitchell smiled. "Have you decided on the type of handgun you want?"

"Not really," Yvette replied. "Any advice on what would be best for me?"

"I'm about to leave here in a minute, how about a cup of coffee, latte, or frappuccino at the coffee house next door and we can talk about it?" Mitchell asked. "I know you're just getting off work and if it's too much, maybe we can do it another time."

"I have a few minutes," Yvette said. "Besides, I only live about five minutes away from here."

"Okay, cool. Give me about five minutes. Let me wrap up a few things and I will meet you there," Mitchell said.

Yvette left the gun range and went three doors down to the coffee shop, grabbed a mocha Frappuccino, and took a seat on the patio of the coffee shop. Soon after, Mitchell walked up. He went in, grabbed an expresso, and joined her.

"Looks like it's going to rain, huh?" he said as he looked up at the sky.

"Yeah, it does," Yvette replied. They sat and talked for what seemed like hours. Mitchell turned out to be a sweet guy. He had kind eyes and a warm smile. She had to keep reminding herself that he was too short for her. She also believed he was a little too straight-edged, the type of guy that would let an alpha female such as herself, run all over him. But he was definitely someone to keep on hand for great convo. And who knows, maybe God blessed him with length in other areas since He forgot to bless him in the height department. The rain came down softly as the two sat on the patio and carried on conversations concerning life, career, and relationships. It was so surreal and pleasant. After a while she said, "I better get going. I have an early morning. It was great talking with you, Mitchell."

"Likewise," he responded. "Let's do it again soon. Maybe we can have some wine at my place instead of coffee," Mitchell added.

"Sounds great, I look forward to it." The two went their separate ways for the evening.

The next morning, Yvette woke up to a text from an unknown number that read, "So, it's like that. You better learn how to shoot and pack that gun everywhere you go or be ready to run when you see me." Yvette was shocked. *Who could have sent such a text and why?* She thought about her ex-husband. The divorce did not end on great terms. She ultimately had to get a restraining order and move away because he was totally against a divorce. Then she thought, *maybe it's Geo.*

She hadn't heard from him since the incident with him and the gun, but no, he wouldn't threaten her like that. Of course, he was upset then, but she believed he would have gotten past it by now. Whoever it was had to be watching her. The texts mentioned learning how to shoot. Someone must have seen her at the gun range.

That day at work, Yvette was paranoid. She looked around and over her shoulder so much it was noticed by her co-workers and her boss. She had taken the gun license class but had not yet purchased a gun. When she left the job that evening, it was dark outside.

Yvette walked out of the building and searched the parking lot. Nervously, she opened her car door and checked the back seat and floor, to make sure no one was inside. She got in quickly and locked the doors. Her phone rang and nearly scared her to death. It was Mitchell.

"Hey, I was hoping I would catch you before you got home. I'm in the middle of cooking and I thought I would call you and invite you over for a glass of wine and to see if you were hungry."

"Yeah, sure," Yvette said.

"What's wrong?" Mitchell asked. He sensed tension in Yvette's voice.

"Mitchell, I may need to borrow one of your guns."

"What, why, what's wrong?" he asked.

"I will talk to you about it once I get there."

"Okay, I'll text you my address." After she received the text she programmed it into her GPS.

It took about 20 minutes before Yvette arrived at Mitchell's home. Yvette got out of the car and rang the doorbell. Mitchell opened the door with a look of concern.

"Come in and have a seat. Here's a glass of wine. Now what's going on?"

"I woke up this morning to a weird and threatening text," Yvette began. "It kinda has me shook up. I couldn't concentrate at work today. My entire day was thrown off. Whoever it is knows that I took your class."

"Who could it be, and why would they be threatening you?" Mitchell asked.

"I have had a couple of bad breakups, one of which was a marriage. The second one ended about three months ago. It was a guy I had been dating on and off for the past three years. Neither ended well, but the last relationship, he basically told me I would see him again. He hasn't called nor have I seen him but those words have always stuck in the back of my mind. Now after taking your class and having coffee with you, I'm all of a sudden getting a threatening text."

"I definitely have a gun you can borrow, if you feel unsafe."

"Thank you," Yvette said. "It will be until I can purchase my own."

"I have an arsenal of guns. I collect them. I'm ex-military. Let's go take a look. You can keep one as long as you need it. Come upstairs, and let me see what you can handle."

Yvette eyes grew big and a smile came across her face. "I'm talking about guns." Mitchell smiled when he saw Yvette's facial expression. "I keep them in the closet in my spare room. Grab your wine and come on up."

Yvette followed Mitchell upstairs into the spare room. He opened up the closet and sure enough, there was an arsenal featuring guns in every size.

"What catches your attention?" he asked.

Yvette picked up a black medium-sized gun. It was sleek, not too heavy and not too light in weight.

"I like this one," she said.

"That may be a little much for you to handle. That's a 9 mm Ruger. Why don't you try this one."

Mitchell handed her a smaller gun. "This is a 22. It's a little smaller and you can fit it in your purse. It's also easier to conceal."

"No, I want the 9," she said. "Please, Mitchell?" She gave him a doe-eyed look while batting her long lashes. Yvette could tell he was totally into her and she used it to her advantage.

"Okay," Mitchell said. "Let me give you a little breakdown of how to handle this gun before you take it with you."

He went over the gun's functions, how to load it, unload it, safety features, how to check the chamber and how to hold it.

"You got it?" he asked.

"Yes," Yvette replied. "Hopefully I won't have to use it."

"If it comes down to them or you, you better not hesitate," Mitchell replied. "You hungry? The food is done."

"Not really. I had a big lunch, and I try not to eat too late. Thanks, so much Mitchell."

Yvette gave him a hug. With that embrace, Mitchell wrapped his arms around Yvette's waist and hugged her tight and held her for a second before he let her go. He was definitely trying to send a signal. Yvette sensed it but brushed it off.

"Goodnight, Mitchell."

"Goodnight, Yvette." Mitchell stood in the doorway of his home and watched her as she got into the car and drove away.

The next morning, Yvette woke up to another threatening text: "That mother fucker will not be able to protect you, you better watch your back, I'm everywhere you are."

Yvette couldn't believe it. Not again. But this time, Yvette texted back, "fuck you! You don't put fear in my heart you fucking coward!"

She received a reply saying, "LOL, we will see." Yvette was nervous. Although she had protection, fear of the unknown consumed her.

Days went by and periodically she would get a threatening text. Whoever sent them always knew where she was or had been, as if they had been watching her every move.

This fear ultimately caused problems on her job. She couldn't sleep, her job performance suffered, and Yvette experienced anxiety attacks to the point she had to be medicated again. That was something she had worked hard to overcome after her divorce. Then calls started coming in to her job where someone would ask for her and then not say anything.

"Yvette, can you come to my office please?" The voice on the intercom of Yvette's office phone brought her out of the daze she was in. It was her boss.

"I will be right there," Yvette said. She gathered her thoughts and went into her boss's office.

"Yes, Rachel?"

"Have a seat," her boss said. "Look, Yvette I don't know what's going on lately. The numbers in your department have dropped drastically. You have been inconsistent in finishing products, you're late getting into work, and you're here, but you're not present. Your department is suffering and it's going to take a miracle to pull it out of the deficit it is in right now." She took a deep breath. "We're going to have to let you go. I have noticed a change in you and if you can work through that, I will be glad to have the old Yvette back. She was a go-getter who ran the highest performance in the company."

"Please! I'm sorry. I have been going through so much, I promise I will get it together. Rachel, I really need my job," Yvette pleaded.

"I can offer you two months severance, but because of whatever you're dealing with your performance has suffered greatly and it's costing the company a lot of money."

"I have busted my ass for this company!" Yvette yelled. "And the minute I fall off because I'm going through something this is the thanks I get! Someone is threatening my life. Okay? Of course, I can't focus or concentrate. Someone is watching my every move."

"I will suggest you go to the police," Rachel said.

"I've done that. I don't know who it is and unless he does something to me they told me there's nothing they can do," she sobbed.

"Calm down, Yvette. I'm sorry. It's out of my hands." Yvette walked back to her desk, grabbed her purse, and stormed out of the door with tears running down her face. She sat in the car shaking and sobbing uncontrollably. She began to hyperventilate. She reached for her anxiety meds. A few minutes went by and she calmed down. She had to get herself together. She needed to figure out her next move. She couldn't just fall apart because Jayden and Katrina needed her. She wiped her tears and drove directly to the unemployment office to apply for assistance. She hoped there would not be much of a break in income until she could find something else.

Yvette walked into the unemployment office, looked around, and could not believe she was there. She had not been out of work since she was in her early 20s when Katrina was about two or three years old. Yvette had always prided herself on working hard and not taking handouts. She was next in line to sit and talk with someone and turn in her paperwork. She looked around and the majority of the people there *looked* unemployed. Yvette sat down to speak with the woman at the desk and after a couple of words, she burst into tears. *How could I let myself end up here?*

The woman at the desk looked at her and asked, "What's wrong ma'am?"

"I shouldn't be here," Yvette managed to say through tears and sniffles.

The woman looked Yvette up and down. She was still wearing her business suit and heels from the office. The lady rested her hands on top of Yvette's hands in an effort to calm her down and said, "You paid into this. This is here for you on such occasions. Don't feel bad about receiving it until you get on your feet. It's yours and I don't see you being the type to stay on assistance for long. Things happen. That's why programs like this are in place. Don't feel ashamed."

Yvette managed to look up at the woman and saw that she smiled at her with a look of comfort and assurance. Yvette felt a sense of peace come over her. On the drive home, she thought about what she was going to tell the kids. *What if they have to move because unemployment isn't enough to cover the bills.* "Oh, Lord, I need to get a drink. I got to get this off my mind," she said aloud. Yvette picked up the phone and dialed Kelsey's number.

"Girl, I need to get out for a drink," Yvette said.

"Why, what's wrong?" Kelsey asked.

"Girl, I got fired today."

"Fired? How?"

"Girl, it's a long story. Can you meet me at Los Cucos for a margarita in the next 30 minutes? I really need a drink before I have a nervous breakdown."

"Yeah, I can be there in 30 minutes. Did you call Elisha, or do you want me to?" Kelsey asked.

"No, no, I'm really not up for the sarcasm right now," Yvette replied.

"Okay, see you in 30 minutes."

"Thanks, see you in a bit." The two met up at a local Mexican restaurant called Los Cucos restaurant and bar. They sat and talked and Yvette told Kelsey everything that's been going on. Even what transpired with Geo and the gun.

"Oh, my goodness! Why have you been keeping all of this to yourself?" Kelsey asked. "No wonder you're about to lose your damn mind. You should have talked to one of us."

"Girl, it got so bad I went and borrowed one of Mitchell's guns."

"Wait, what? Mitchell? Mitchell from the handgun class? The instructor?"

"Oh yeah, I forgot to mention we have hung out a few times."

"Oh, really? Give me all the details."

Kelsey leaned forward with her chin resting on her hand.

"There are no details, we just had coffee one day then he invited me over for a glass of wine and that's when I picked up the gun. Nothing more."

"Hmmmmmm … why not? He's a good-looking guy. He's nice, educated, owns his own business, and has a phenomenal body. What's the problem?"

"Nothing, I'm just not interested in him that way. Besides it's only been four months since my breakup with Geo. I don't want to treat him like a rebound."

"You know what they say, 'the best cure to get over an old dick, is to get some new dick.'"

"Girl stop, I'm not interested, and besides he's short."

"You're short!"

"Exactly! We are going to look like we escaped from the Lollipop Guild from The Wizard of Oz." Kelsey laughed so hard she spit Margarita everywhere.

"No, you did not say that!" she laughed.

When the drinks and food came, they talked and laughed more. It took Yvette's mind off her current state of affairs. The two were having such a great time, before they knew it was midnight.

"Okay, chick, I got to go," Kelsey said. Some of us have a job to go to in the morning," she laughed. Yvette's demeanor became somber."Oh, lighten up, Yvette, it's not the end of the world. You're a boss ass bitch. You will bounce back. It's not the end of the world. You're going to be fine."

Yvette's phone rang. It was Mitchell. She told Kelsey and said she would call him later.

"Girl, answer that phone and go over there and get some medicine. I promise you it will take your mind off everything and relax you in the process." She winked.

"I am feeling some type of way with all these margaritas I drank." She answered the phone.

"Hey, Yvette, I just passed by Los Cucos and I thought I saw your car," Mitchell said.

"Yeah, I'm hanging out with Kel's," she replied. "You know, just a little girl chit chat."

"Oh, where are you headed to after that?" Mitchell asked.

"Dealing with a lot right now, I was just going to go home."

"You know you're not far from my house. If you've had a little too much to drink you can come over and rest or talk. I'm always here for you if you need to talk, Yvette."

Yvette looked up at Kelsey and nodded her head.

"Actually, I will take you up on that. I am leaving here in about five minutes."

"Okay, I will see you then. Do you still remember how to get here or do you need me to come back and guide you?"

"Yes, I remember, and no I'll be just fine." Yvette hung up the phone.

"Oh, my God, I can't believe I agreed to go over there. It's after midnight. He's going to be expecting something. What if I am feeling it when I get there?"

"Girl, stop overthinking it and go and get some medicine, because I'm about to go get mine. He's actually not with his baby mama tonight, so I got to go! Smooches, call me and give me all the details tomorrow!"

Kelsey scampered off to her car in a haste. Yvette stopped in the restaurant bathroom on the way to her car to check her makeup and hair to make sure she didn't look too drunk. After a few touch ups and a cup of water to go, she headed to her car. Yvette's mind was in a totally different zone. For the moment, she was not thinking about the phone calls, threats, and texts.

She focused on one thing and that was to relieve some of the tension, and hoping she was not disappointed. Her phone chimed from a text coming in to her phone. It was Mitchell letting her know the door wold be unlocked and he would be upstairs. Yvette took a deep breath and started on her way to Mitchell's house.

She arrived at his town home. Like he said, the door was unlocked. Yvette walked up stairs and he was lying across the bed watching TV.

"I have had a day from hell, let me just say that for starters," Yvette exclaimed.

"Take your shoes off, lay across the bed and relax and tell me all about it," Mitchell replied.

"I lost my job. This whole thing with my ex and the unknown calls and texts have really taken a toll on me."

"I'm here for you if you need anything, and I'm so sorry you lost your job, but you're smart, you're talented, you're a go-getter, not to mention you are extremely gorgeous. You will find something better."

"Thank you, Mitchell. You're sweet." *Gosh, he's cute and sweet, why couldn't he just be six feet tall?*

"Lie on your stomach, and let me give you a massage."

"A massage?"

"I'm also a licensed masseuse. I don't practice it as much as I used to, but I haven't lost my touch."

Yvette said, "I could definitely use that."

He rolled her over on her stomach and Mitchell began to give her a massage. He started from her shoulders and went all the way down to her feet. He left leaving no spot untouched. His gentle but firm hands gripped her small waistline while his thumbs deeply massaged her spine.

"Turnover," Mitchell said. *Turn over? What is he going to massage if I turn over?* Nevertheless she turned over and Mitchell proceeded to massage her shoulders and arms one by one all the way to her fingertips. Yvette lay there with her eyes closed with the reflection from the TV bouncing off her skin in the darkness. He massaged her inner and outer thighs. This made Yvette tingle all over. He finished it up by massaging her neck and scalp, then her temples. He gave her a kiss on the forehead to end it all. She opened her eyes to see Mitchell staring down at her and she smiled nervously.

"That was nice, thank you."

"You're welcome." Mitchell laid next to Yvette and cuddled her. It felt nice, but Yvette wondered why he didn't try anything after all of that touching. They laid there until the both of them fell asleep. Early that morning, before daylight, Yvette got up to use the restroom. When she came back to the bed Mitchell was awake.

"How did you sleep?" he asked.

"Great. With the margaritas I had and that massage you gave me. Thanks again. I needed that."

"You're welcome. I got you anytime you need one."

"I'm going to get going. I don't want to do the Walk of Shame when I get home and my children are awake. She actually felt disappointed because there was another way she would have liked to relieve some stress and tension.

"Oh, I was hoping I could make you some breakfast," Mitchell said.

"That's okay," Yvette said.

Mitchell was disappointed.

He said, "Let me walk you out."

They got to the door and Yvette turned around and said, "I appreciate you so much Mitchell for everything," and gave him a hug. He hugged her back, but held on to her while pressing his body firmly against her body. He pulled back, looked her in her eyes and kissed her deeply and aggressively. The thoughts of going home and the dreaded walk of shame soon left. This felt good and it was what she wanted and needed.

"Do you want me to stop?" Mitchell asked.

Breathlessly, Yvette whispered, "no."

Mitchell then lifted Yvette off her feet and carried her back upstairs. This not only impressed Yvette, but it was a major turn on. He laid her gently on the bed and began to undress her, kissing her as he went. He removed his shirt and shorts and climbed onto the bed kissing every inch of her body. He flipped her over on her stomach and dragged his tongue down her spine biting her on her behind. Yvette could not believe the level of passion he possessed. He gently turned her over once more and looked into her eyes, but he never said a word. He kissed her forehead again, then went down her neck and back up. He devoured her mouth.

He looked at her and her eyes and said, "You don't know I have desired you from the moment I laid eyes on you."

He began to penetration her. Much to Yvette's surprise and pleasure this was not a smooth process. God actually did make up for his height in other ways. The intensity drove Yvette crazy. Sweat from his body rain down on her body and face. Everything went great, the passion inflamed, but Yvette struggled to stay in the moment in spite of the torrential rain of sweat dripping down on her. She managed to release with a loud moan and at the same time he did.

Afterwards they lay there for a moment. Finally, Mitchell got up and turned on the shower. He called for her to join him and he slowly washed her body from head to toe before washing his own body. After the shower, he dried her off and put lotion on her body. Yvette loved that he was attentive and caring.

"I'm going to make some breakfast. How do you like your eggs?" Mitchell asked.

"I really should be going. I know my children are awake by now."

"Just tell them you had a few drinks and didn't want to drive home, so you stayed at a friend's house. I'm sure they will respect that."

"Yeah, that's a good excuse," Yvette laughed

Mitchell walked her to the door. "I really hope you enjoyed me as much as I enjoyed you," he said.

"I did. It was what I really needed."

"I hope it won't be the last time," he said and brushed her hair across her forehead with his hand. Yvette gave him another hug. Yvette got into her car, pulled down the visor and looked in the mirror.

"Oh, my goodness! I look a mess!" she exclaimed. "Being too drunk to drive is one thing, but how do I explain my hair and makeup looking like I have been caught in a hurricane?"

Yvette used her long nails like a comb to smooth down her black tresses of hair as much as she could. She opened her glove compartment to retrieve some leftover napkins she had saved from lunch to fix her smudged make up.

She arrived home at 10 a.m. It was Sunday morning so she knew the children were home and awake. She opened the door and Katrina and Jaden sat on the sofa looking upset and sad. Katrina asked, "Mom where were you?"

"I stayed at a friend's house because I had a few drinks and didn't want to drive."

"We have been trying to reach you. We called your phone several times but it kept going to voicemail."

"What?" Yvette exclaimed.

She rummaged through her purse for her phone, and found that it was indeed dead as a door nail.

She had not told the children that she had lost her job so she couldn't imagine why they were looking so sad and distraught. "I didn't know my phone had died, what's wrong?" Katrina began to sob uncontrollably.

"We tried to call you all night, because Auntie Cara called and said our great grandma passed away last night," Jaden said sadly. Yvette could not believe her ears. Her Grandma Martha had been battling Alzheimer's for a while, along with a couple of other old age ailments. They had just celebrated her 90th birthday and was preparing for the 91st. Yvette was hurt. Her grandmother was everything to her and she taught her everything she knew as a little girl, like how to cook and how to sew. She was always there for them when her mom couldn't provide for them as children. Cookouts, holidays and family events would never be the same. When it rains it most certainly pours.

"What's next! My heart can't take anymore!" Yvette cried out. Jaden did not hear what she said but Katrina wondered what she meant by that.

Later that day, Yvette called and spoke with her sister and the rest of the family to find out information concerning the funeral arrangements. That night, Yvette lay awake in bed thinking about her life and wondering what did she do to go through so much at once. The only positive thing in her life at this moment was a voicemail she received asking her to come in for an interview at a local Fortune 500 company. Even that didn't stop the tears. She laid there and cried so much her pillow became soaked in tears. She cried herself to sleep.

The next morning, Yvette awakened and got dressed to go on the job interview. In spite of everything going on she knew she had to pull it together. She had to get another job and take care of her family. Katrina would be going off to college in a couple of months and she would need support. Then it would be time for Jaden's prom and graduation, being that they were three years apart. This was not the time to fall completely apart. She got dressed, flawlessly put her makeup on and curled her hair. She gave herself a once-over in the mirror and she could hear her Grandma's voice telling her "don't ever look like what you're going through," and "don't accept any wooden nickels." That made her smile. Yvette grabbed her purse, got in her car, and set off on her interview. As she neared her destination she stopped for a red light. When it turned green, she pressed the gas pedal but the car seemed to be stuck in one speed and would not accelerate over 20 miles per hour. Cars zoomed past her and angry drivers honked their horns. *What in the hell could be going on now?* "Oh, please God not my car!" she shouted.

CHAPTER 9
PAYING RESPECTS AND LETTING GO

Yvette was alone with her thoughts. *Next weekend my grandmother will be laid to rest, the matriarch of my life and the family. My car is in the shop, I have no job, and I'm low on money. I have to get to my grandmother's funeral. Maybe I can get a payday loan. Oh, hell, I guess first I would need a job. Why is all of this happening at once?*

Her phone rang. It was Mitchell. "Hey, what's going on? he asked, I haven't heard anything from you since the other night. Did I do something wrong? Did we move too fast? Hell, was the sex bad?"

"Everything between us is fine Mitchell. When I got home after being with you, I found out my children had been trying to get in touch with me because my grandma passed away. They couldn't reach me because my phone was dead."

"I'm so sorry for your loss," he responded.

"And to top it off, on my way to a job interview my car started acting up. Needless to say I never made it to the interview. I'm still jobless, my car is in the shop getting the transmission repaired, I have to go pick up a rental to pay my respects to my grandmother and be with my family and I'm low on funds until my unemployment hits. It's too much. I don't know how much more I can take."

"Do you need some money to help out?" Mitchell asked.

"I can't take money from you, Mitchell. I will work it out."

"Yvette, I don't mind. Let me help you. It can be a loan if you want, Pay it back when you can, if that makes you feel better."

Although Yvette did not want to take money from Mitchell, it was her only other option besides not going at all and she could never let her grandmother be buried without her being there.

She agreed. "It will be a loan. I will pay you back as soon as I get stable."

"I'm not worried," Mitchell said. "When will you pick up the rental?"

"I'm going to pick it up Thursday night and head out Friday morning. The funeral is on Saturday."

"Just let me know what time you want to go and I will take you to pick up the rental."

"Thank you, Mitchell. You have no idea how much I appreciate that. I'm about to lose my mind, so much is coming at me at once."

"I understand but just know I got you. I'm here for you. All you have to do is let me know."

"I appreciate that," Yvette replied.

The funeral came and went and just as promised, Mitchell was there for Yvette. He drove her to the airport to pick up the rental and put $500 cash in her hand for whatever she needed when she got there. After the funeral was over, Yvette came back down to reality. No job and rent was due in a couple of weeks, but at least her car was fixed and unemployment payments were about to start.

The doorbell rang. "I'm coming!" Yvette hollered.

She opened the door and saw Kelsey and Elisha standing there.

"No, we didn't call first, because we didn't think you would answer. How are you holding up?" Elisha asked.

"I'm okay. I'm just in here on the internet. I uploaded some résumés. Come on in."

"You need to get out and let loose, and forget about your troubles for a minute," Elisha said.

"Why is that always your remedy?" Kelsey laughed.

"What better way to take your mind off your problems than to find a few men, some drinks, and good music," Elisha said as she danced around provocatively.

"Girl!" Yvette laughed.

"At least she got you to laugh," Kelsey said. "Speaking of men, how did things go with you and Mitchell the other night?"

"What?" Elisha shouted. "You and Mitchell?"

"Oh, my God, why did you have to mention that in front of her? Geesh!"

"Oh no! But you said he was too short!" Elisha said loudly.

"He is short but he's sweet and we are only friends. He helped me release some tension that night, but besides that, I'm not looking for anything. I just got out of a situation and I don't want another one right now."

"Okay," whatever," Kelsey said. "I don't care about that, just give me the details! Was it good?"

"Let's just say big things sometimes come in small packages!" Yvette said.

"Really?" Kelsey's eyes grew with intrigue.

"It was nice. It started off with a massage and a forehead kiss at first and we fell asleep."

"Forehead kiss!" Elisha shouted.

"Oh damn, he really likes you."

"Why do you say that? Because he kissed her on the forehead?" Kelsey asked.

"Yeah, it's a sign of endearment," Elisha explained.

"Wow, I never knew that. Damn it. Now you are going to have me looking for forehead kisses and shit," Kelsey yelled.

They all laughed hysterically.

"Look, come on Yvette. I know you're going through a lot, but let's just get out for a minute and forget about it just for tonight," Elisha said. "There's an all white party at Club Ignite tonight and besides we all haven't been out together because you were all caught up with Geo and kicked us to the curb."

"God don't mention his name too loudly. I still think he's the one that has been sending me crazy texts, called my job, and caused me to get fired."

"Wait, what crazy text messages? Who was calling your job? And when did you get fired? You bitches been keeping secrets," Elisha said pointing her finger.

"We know how you over act and get loud," Kelsey said.

"You're right. Let's go out. I need to get away and take my mind off things."

"Wait, before we leave," Elisha said. You say big things come in small packages, huh? I want to know how big was it? Stand up and walk to the door and let me see if you are walking differently."

"Girl, you are crazy!" Yvette laughed. "It was a nice size, trust me. There was only one thing that turned me off. Once we got into it and he was on top, he sweated profusely!"

"Damn, he must have been doing the damn thing, but what's wrong with a little sweat?" Elisha asked.

"Girl, did you not hear me say profusely? I'm talking almost thunderstorm like dripping in my eyes and hair. I couldn't get into it as much as I wanted to because I spent the majority of the time wiping sweat from his face so it wouldn't drip in my eye!"

"Damn, I bet your walk of shame the next morning had to be horrendous," Kelsey said shaking her head.

"Yeah, needless to say it was," Yvette said what a sigh. "It was."

Later that night they met up at Club Ignite. When they walked in there was a sea of people in white everywhere. The fact that Yvette loves dress theme parties helped. The trio made their way to the bar and ordered drinks. They then made their way to a table. The music was pumped up and beautiful people were all over the place, some with accent-colored shoes and some completely adorned in white from head to toe. Yvette wore a white pair of skinny jeans that hugged her curves and accentuated her thighs and butt, with a see-through white lace top, and a white bustier underneath. Since her favorite color is purple, she accented her feet with a pair of purple stiletto strappy heels. Curly hair flowed down her back, and her makeup and nails were on fleek. Yvette was ready to forget about her woes, at least for tonight and enjoy herself.

"Get it then bitch, you look cute," Elisha said.

"Thank you, girl," Yvette responded.

"Any torrential rain in the forecast tonight after the club?" Elisha laughed.

"Shut up Elisha. That's why I never tell you anything."

"I'm just playing. Loosen up. That's the whole purpose of coming out tonight, right? To forget and let loose."

"She's right," Kelsey said. "Let loose and take your mind off everything for a minute. I still see stress in your face. Let It Go!"

"Awwwwww shit, that's my song! Okay, girls I'm about to go sexy dance in the mirror and hope some fine, well-to-do guy is watching and wants to wife me so I don't have to work anymore," Elisha said and strutted off to the dance floor.

Yvette said, Kelsey, I really like this spot and you know my birthday is coming up.

This would be a nice place to have a party."

"The owner's name is Travis. Sometimes he passes through. If I see him tonight, I'll introduce you and you can speak to him about it. In the meantime, let's join Elisha's crazy-ass on the dance floor and dance away your troubles."

"Okay," Yvette said. "Stressing about it doesn't make it better no ways."

Kelsey and Yvette made their way to the dance floor and the drinks started to kick in. Soon, Yvette troubles began to get lost in song and she moved and gyrated her hips ever so fluently to the beat of Beyonce's song, "Check on It."

Yvette watched herself in the mirror and enjoyed her own moves. She noticed someone else watched her, as well. A man leaned against the bar and wore a white suit jacket, button down shirt, white slacks, and white shoes against the backdrop of his dark chocolate skin. He stood six foot tall and had a freshly cut waves on swim. Yvette couldn't help but notice him as he watched her. She began to gyrate harder and more seductively, and ran her hands through her long hair and then down her body. She gave him something to look at. After a while, the trio made their way back to their section of the club, but not before Yvette made eye contact with the handsome stranger and smiled. The song ended and she walked back to her table.

"Bitch! What were you doing out there? Channeling your inner stripper," Elisha asked.

"You sure took sexy dancing in the mirror to another level out there. No more drinks for you, Chocolate Delight. That's your stripper name," Kelsey laughed.

"What?" Yvette exclaimed. I was just feeling the music."

"Yeah, right," Elisha responded as she sipped her drink. Yvette scanned the club for the handsome stranger and could not find him anywhere. She was about to give up. She thought maybe she had imagined him being there when she spotted him sitting in a VIP section along with a group of other guys and a couple of ladies.

"Hey, who is that guy over there in the VIP by the bar?" Yvette asked.

"Which guy?" Elisha asked.

There are a lot of them over there."

"The chocolate one with the perfectly formed waves and …"

Before she could finish her thoughts, Elisha responded with, "Oh hell! Say no more. You must be talking about Dalvin, the concert promoter. Why are you asking about him?"

"I saw him watching me."

"Oh, that's why you were being extra on the dance floor, huh?"

"No," Yvette smirked.

"Girl, you don't want that trust me. That dick is for everybody. He doesn't want anything serious. You know he gets so much pussy thrown at him on a regular, you do not want to be in that number."

"I think he is sexy as hell that's all. I'll be right back."

Yvette made her way to the restroom. Once she finished, she washed her hands, checked her hair and makeup and reapplied her lipstick. As she made her way across the dance floor, her hips simultaneously swung and shifted to the beat of the music without effort. Lights bounced off the silhouette of her body. She felt a tug at her hand. Yvette turned around and there standing before her with a perfectly trimmed goatee around a pair of the sexiest lips, looking like chocolate draped in milk, was Mr. Waves on Swim, Dalvin, smelling delicious and looking like a whole meal.

"Are you married?" he asked, in the sexiest voice that Yvette had ever heard.

His eyes were light brown and accented by thick eyebrows. Yvette felt like they pierced her soul. She managed to break out of her trance and say, "No, I'm not."

"What are you drinking?" he asked.

"Chardonnay," she replied shyly. He ordered a glass of Chardonnay from the bar and the two stood there and talked. Dalvin asked the majority of the questions. Yvette stood there mesmerized by his charm.

Eventually he said, "I'm going to let you get back to your friends. I'm here almost every Saturday if I'm not on the road promoting a concert or something. I hope I see you again."

"It's a possibility." Yvette smiled as she walked away and headed back to the table where Kelsey and Elisha sat. As she walked towards the table, she could see the two ladies staring piercingly at her.

"What?" Yvette asked.

"You insist on jumping on the Dalvin train, huh?" Kelsey said.

"Girl, he bought me a drink, geesh!"

"That's how he gets you. That smile, those light brown eyes, conversation layered in charm and bullshit," Elisha said.

"You walked back over here with stars in your damn, eyes."

"Girl, stop it. It's not that serious," Yvette said. "We had a conversation that's it. We didn't even change numbers."

"All he wants to do is fuck. He see some new booty in the club."

"Maybe that's all I want, too," Yvette said.

"Girl, you better keep your game face on with that one!" Elisha said.

"Wait, what about Mitchell?" Kelsey asked.

"What do you mean?" Yvette replied.

"He seems to really like you."

"Okay, and?" Yvette said. "I'm not obligated to him. We are just friends. He's a sweet man, but I'm not looking to get into anything serious and he seems to be getting a little too attached. Besides if I ever feel like making love in the rain without actually being outside in it I know who to call."

"Bitch you better wrap your hair and put a plastic cap on your head the next time!" Elisha laughed loudly. They all laugh uncontrollably and headed back to the dance floor for one last dance before ending the night.

CHAPTER 10
THE DALVIN FACTOR

The next day, Yvette could not get Dalvin's piercing brown eyes, those sexy lips, and his swagger off her mind. She laid awake in bed that morning, and her mind wandered all over the place. She wondered what *it* would be like. She didn't get his number that night and for the first time ever, she felt the desire to pursue a man. Her grandma always told her a man was supposed to pursue a woman and not the other way around, but she could not get him off her mind. She had to see him again. Yvette visited Club Ignite for the next couple of Saturdays, hoping to run into him again, but he was not there either time. Yvette had never been a person to frequent the clubs back to back, so Kelsey and Elisha knew what was up.

"I have a question. How is it that all of a sudden your ass want to hit the club every weekend, huh?" Elisha asked.

"Girl, you know I got a lot on my mind. I'm just trying to keep all the idle time filled."

"Yeah, right bitch. Your ass been stung by the Dalvin bug. That Charming motherfucker has gotten you."

"No he didn't," Yvette said.

"Look at me," Kelsey said.

Yvette turned to look at Kelsey. "Oh, yeah. She's gone."

"Stop it, you guys. I mean the brother is fine. I only want to see what he's working with. I mean what has got these women so crazy about him? He walks to the club and they stop him and grab at him and try to get his attention."

"Oh, so you want to be one of them?" Kelsey asked.

"Child, I could never be that," Yvette responded.

"If you feel some type of way about him I say go for it, step to him. Often women wait to get chosen. Choose his ass. You already know what's up. Just don't get caught up," Kelsey said.

"Look what I see here. Here is a flyer for a concert with all of his info on it. I say give him a call."

Kelsey picked up the flyer that seemed to be conveniently left at every table. Yvette took the flyer but could not fathom the idea of making the first move and calling a man first. She thought to herself, *hell I have been having the worst luck being chosen. Maybe my luck would be better if I did the choosing. After all, I know what he's all about and I will play the game however it goes.*

A few weeks went by. Yvette stopped visiting the club as much because she finally got a new job and she wanted everything to go well. The Fortune 500 company was so impressed with her résumé that they gave her a second shot at another interview. She also never stopped thinking about Dalvin.

One evening, she made the decision that she would make that move. She looked through her purse for the flyer and couldn't seem to find it. Feverishly, she searched in every crevice and pocket inside her purse. Finally, she dumped it out on the bed and found the flyer under a stack of receipts, lipstick, lip gloss tubes, and sticks of gum. She picked up the phone and started to call but before she dialed his number, she practiced how she would talk and what she would initially say to him.

He didn't give her his number, what would be her reason for calling him? She couldn't just pick up the phone and say, "Hi my name is Yvette. You remember me from the club? Oh yeah, by the way I heard you are quite the ladies man and I want to find out why."

Naah. *What do I say? You know what? I'm going to do it*, she said to herself. Yvette picked up the phone and her heart pounded nervously as she dialed the number on the flyer.

"This is Dalvin speaking can I help you?" Yvette's voice trembled.

"Hi, Dalvin, this is Yvette. I met you at Club Ignite about a month ago at an all-white affair. She began to describe herself to help jog his memory, because she was sure he had met several women that night and even more since then.

He responded, "Say no more. How can I forget you? What's up, gorgeous?" Yvette smiled as if he stood right in front of her.

"I know you are promoting the concert that's coming, and I was wondering where to get the best tickets for the best price?"

Dalvin named several available sections in the arena where the artists would be more visible, that was not so pricey. Then he stopped and said, "I tell you what. Why don't you be my guest for that night? I can get you backstage and you can see how I work."

"Wow!"Yvette responded. I was only calling to get info and I got something even better. I will be glad to be your guest." This is not what she had in mind but she figured she would play coy for now.

After a couple of weeks, the job was going great, and the children were doing well. Jaden's prom was over. Katrina was doing exceptional in college and there were not any more texts or phone calls from the anonymous psycho. Yvette felt like she could finally breathe and not have to watch her back.

CHAPTER 11
DANCING WITH THE DEVIL #DALVIN

The day of the concert, Dalvin and Yvette decided that she would meet him at his hotel and that they would take a private car to the arena in case they wanted to drink. Also it was because Dalvin always like to make an entrance. Dalvin called Yvette and said, "I'm going to be at the venue checking some things out prior to the concert. I will leave a key for you at the front desk. You can go to the room, shower, and change if you like. I will be there shortly after."

"Sounds great," Yvette agreed.

Once Yvette got to the hotel she went to the front desk and Dalvin had indeed left her key as he said. Upon entering the hotel room, Yvette noticed that Dalvin had left out a bottle of Chardonnay and a couple of wine glasses. *Wow, he remembered,* she thought.

He also left her a note that read:

"I bought you your favorite bottle. Have a glass, relax, and I'll see you soon."

Yvette did just that. She poured a glass of wine, took a few sips, and ran a hot shower. Yvette got out the shower and started to get dressed. Midway, she decided to give Kelsey and Elisha a call to give them the four-one-one on where she was.

"Bitch! How are you not going to get us tickets, too," Elisha shouted. "I can't believe you. You are so selfish."

"Shut up, Elisha!" Kelsey said. "Are you going to give up some ass for some tickets?"

"Hell, no," Elisha shouted. That dick for everybody, and I mean everybody."

"It's going to be for Yvette tonight because that's what she wants, right Yvette?" Kelsey stated.

"Yeah I guess," Yvette replied.

"What do you mean you guess? You're in that man's hotel room and he got you backstage passes to a concert your thinking is over, boo." Yvette heard someone at the door.

"Okay you guys, I got to go. I think he's here."

Before Yvette hung up the phone she could hear Elisha shout, "Keep your game face on bitch!"

The door opened and he stood there suited and booted. He wore a black Brooks Brothers suit with a matching vest, red tie, with a red mult-colored pocket square, white shirt underneath, and reddish brown Allen Edmonds shoes. Yvette took a deep breath and said, "You look handsome."

"You look amazing as well, and what a coincidence, Lady in Red, I love that dress. You're wearing the hell out of it!" He circled Yvette and looked her up and down. The dress was form-fitting down to the knee. It was low-cut in the front and backless with a red pair of strappy stilettos to match. She gave the reverse effect of a chocolate covered strawberry ... a strawberry covered chocolate ... and Dalvin stared at her like he wanted a bite.

They got to the concert rather early. Yvette was given a backstage tour and got the opportunity to watch Dalvin in action. Although he was in work mode, he was attentive to her and showed her off.

He introduced her to his friends and people backstage and also watched her from a distance while he maneuvered backstage to keep everything going.

The concert was awesome although Dalvin didn't get an opportunity to sit with her much. She still had a great time. Back in the car on the way to the hotel, he apologized for not being able to spend much time with her during the concert.

"No need to apologize, I understand," Yvette said. "I appreciated the invite. I've never been backstage at a concert before."

The car pulled up to the hotel. "I had a great time," Yvette said. "Oh, wait, I left my bag with my other clothes. I need to come up and get them. They went upstairs to the hotel room so that Yvette could retrieve her bag. She grabbed her bag and was about to exit the hotel room door. She thanked him again for a great time, all the while in the back of her mind, she wondered what *it* would be like. Her intentions were not a concert; they were to be bold and choose to do what she wanted with this man on her own terms, but she got scared.

Before she could open the door, Dalvin said, "What? No hug?" He stood there with his shirt un-tucked and his suit jacket off, as if he had already begun to get comfortable.

Yvette responded, "Of course."

She then walked towards Dalvin and wrapped her arms around his neck. He put both hands around her waist and pulled her closer. Yvette's heart beat faster and she became intoxicated by his cologne and high off the feel of his body pressed against hers. As they both relinquished themselves from the embrace, Dalvin kissed Yvette on the forehead. She melted. That was one of her weaknesses. She then looked up at Dalvin with glossy eyes as if she fell in love instantly in that moment, although it didn't make any sense.

"This is not what you want," he said seductively but arrogantly.

She softly asked, "What do you mean?"

"I can tell you want a husband, but I'm not that guy."

"I've had a husband and you're wrong. Been there, done that."

Dalvin smirked, "Yeah, right. I can see it in your eyes."

"Maybe at some point down the line, years from now, yes, I would love to be married again, but right now I only want sex," Yvette spoke boldly.

"Is that right?" Dalvin smiled as if to say now you're speaking my language. He walked up to Yvette, grabbed her by the back of her neck with his right hand, and pulled her close. He passionately kissed her. He utilized the other hand to practically tear her dress off. He pushed her on the bed and she lay there as he stared at her, while undressing himself, not saying a word.

Yvette wasn't used to this type of aggressive sex but she liked it. As the night went on it would get even better. Once Dalvin undressed himself completely, he kneeled down on the floor in front of Yvette, grabbed her by the waist and slid her to the edge of the bed. He forced her legs apart and slid his hand underneath her butt. He began an oral sex session that made Yvette's body convulse like she was having a seizure. He rocked the boat back and forth and bit the inside of her thighs. She arched her back and dug her nails into his shoulders in complete pleasure. Before Yvette could catch her breath, he commanded, "Turn over!"

He traced the cheeks of her butt with his fingertips, then she felt his hot wet tongue run down her spine as he reached underneath her to lift her up to a doggy-style position. He began a slow penetration inside her walls. The fit was snug. He started with slow thrusts, but as condensation began, the more vigorous the thrusts became. Yvette felt pleasure on a totally different level. He took his hand and wrapped it around her throat and begin to squeeze firmly, not to cut off her air supply but to create the ultimate sexual euphoria. She had never been choked while having sex, but the combination was unlike anything she had ever felt. She let out a scream of passion that was sure to be heard by anyone in the adjoining rooms and possibly even in the hallway.

However, he wasn't finished. He turned her over abruptly on her back and began to bite her on the neck, stomach, and then again on her inner thighs. He licked her labia like an animal. She began to pull away; she felt like she was going crazy. She hadn't recovered from the first orgasm. Her head was going to explode.

"Wait," she pleaded.

"No! This is what you wanted, right? Don't run from me." He grabbed Yvette by the waist with her back towards him. He plunged himself deep inside her walls again, and minutes later he erupted. Yvette did also. She felt like she had been in a fight for her life. She laid there for a moment to catch her breath and gather her mindset.

She then went to the bathroom to wash up. When she returned, Dalvin laid sprawled across the bed. He was asleep. Yvette proceeded to put her clothes and shoes on and straightened her hair before she left his hotel room. She tried to look as much as possible like she did when she entered. That wasn't going to happen, but she did her best. Before leaving she tapped Dalvin on the shoulder and let him know she was leaving. He grunted, "okay," but he never moved a muscle. Yvette gathered her things and left.

CHAPTER 12
THE AFTERSHOCK

The next day, Yvette lay in bed all day completely weak and exhausted. She was unable to move. It seemed like her soul had been sucked completely out of her. Never in any of her sexual experiences had she felt this way. It was unexplainable but the reason behind it felt so good. Yvette spent the better part of the day reliving the previous night and replaying it in her head over and over. She hoped she would get a call or text of some sort from Dalvin, but she never did. Days went by, but he didn't call or text. Yvette couldn't get that night out of her mind. Although rough and aggressive, it intrigued her and turned a switch on in her mind and body that she didn't know in that moment she would have hell turning off. She had to get a grip. "Keep your game face on," she kept hearing Elisha say. Yvette wanted to call him. Her body craved him, even if it was only one more time. A couple of weeks went by and Yvette seem to tuck those memories away and move on.

At least she did until girls' night at Club Ignite came again. While sitting in their usual area in the club, Yvette, Elisha, and Kelsey, enjoyed drinks, listened to music, and chair danced as opposed to going on the dance floor. Yvette scanned the room in hopes that Dalvin was in the place somewhere, but she didn't see him. It was already past 11, the usual time he would get to the club, according to those in the know. Then he walked in. Yvette's heart began to flutter and she took a deep breath. She turned her head and tried to be as inconspicuous as possible. She tried to act like that night was nothing, but the mere fact that he was in the building made her body feverish. Yvette tried at every cost to forget that he was there. She laughed extra hard at things that weren't that funny. She drank and gyrated to the beat of the music in her chair. She felt a tap on her shoulder and when she turned around, there he stood with all his armor of sexiness. Yvette felt like her heart stopped. She managed to gather herself and sit up from her chair. She smiled casually as if his presence was like any other guy who approached her.

"How are you doing gorgeous?" Dalvin greeted Yvette with a hug, and pressed his strong fingertips into her as if to remind her of that night. Yvette's knees became weak because that's exactly what it did, remind her of that night. The night she fought hard to get off her mind was brought back to her with only one touch.

He whispered in her ear, "Am I seeing you later?"

She wanted to scream, "Yes! Yes! Yes! Hell, Yes!"

Instead she looked him in his eyes and said "maybe," and smiled wickedly.

He responded, "Okay," then walked away. Yvette sat back down and Elisha stared at her.

"That was a long-ass hug," Elisha said. "What's up with that?"

"Nothing. He gave me a hug," Yvette replied.

"Oh, hell, she's been bit by the Dalvin bug," Kelsey said shaking her head. "I told you to keep your game face on bitch. You over there grinning like Chester Cheetah. Oh damn! Please don't tell me you had sex with that misogynistic fuck boy!" Elisha taunted.

"Wow, Elisha," Kelsey said. "Why that man gotta be all that?"

"Girl a man that has dated and slept with as many women as he has, never married, not one serious relationship on record at his age, is only good for a good fuck, has to hate women. I'm just saying," Elisha explained.

"No, actually we didn't have sex," Yvette lied.

She wouldn't dare tell them what happened that night. They would never let her live it down.

"I thought that's what you said you wanted to do. Didn't you say you wanted to see what he was working with? And why all the girls were so hot and heavy behind him?" Kelsey asked.

"Yeah, I did say that but after the concert, once the car pulled up at the hotel, I got in my car and left. I guess you could say I chickened out."

"It's a good thing you did because from what I heard, chicks get hung up on that dick and I don't know why. I wouldn't want any of it, the way they be acting around here behind him," Elisha said.

"Girl, he's not thug enough for you anyway!" Kelsey said with a laugh.

A few moments later, Mitchell walked up to the table.

"Hey, ladies. How are y'all doing?"

"Hey, Mitchell what are you doing here?"

"I'm here for a birthday party for one of my friends. I saw you ladies over here and thought I would come say hi. Hey, Yvette, you want to dance?" he asked.

From the corner of her eye, she could see Dalvin watching her every move.

"My feet hurt right now. Maybe later," she responded. Kelsey and Elisha gave her the side eye.

"Okay maybe after the club we can go and grab something to eat," Mitchell said. "Yeah, that sounds good," Yvette said.

"Let me get back to the party. I hope to hear from you later, Yvette." She smiled and said, "okay."

"How in the hell do your feet hurt? We have been chair dancing all night," Elisha laughed.

"Shut the hell up," Yvette said.

"He's really a nice guy, Yvette," Kelsey said. "And, he really likes you."

"Yeah, I know I like him, too, but just as a friend."

"That torrential sweat shower during sex turns you off, huh?" Kelsey said. She and Elisha laughed.

"Stop y'all. That's not funny," Yvette said. "That's exactly why I keep certain things to myself."

Once the club closed, Yvette was on her way home when her phone rang. As Yvette scramble to find it, she almost ran off the road trying to retrieve her phone from the bottom of her purse. It was Mitchell calling. She hoped it was Dalvin calling. Yvette got home around 1:30 a.m., showered, and got into bed. She looked at her phone once more before she went to sleep, in case she missed the call while showering. There weren't any missed calls or texts. *It's probably best.* Yvette laid down, closed her eyes and began to drift off to sleep. She received a text notification. She looked at her phone and it was Dalvin. The sleepiness left her body and she became wide awake. The text read, "WYA?"

"At home," Yvette replied. "That's not where you need to be," he replied.

"Then where?" she asked.

"My place. I'm at another spot right now but should be there by the time you make it there. I'm texting you my address."

Without hesitation, Yvette got into her car and was on her way. The distance was almost an hour away, but that didn't matter. Their first sexual encounter was like a drug and she needed to get another fix. Yvette arrived at Dalvin's place. When he opened the door, music played and lighted candles were everywhere. Yvette arrived wearing boy shorts, flip flops, and a tank top, covered by a long sweater. Her hair flowed and she had on a small amount of makeup to keep it cute. Not much conversation went on. Dalvin led Yvette into the bedroom which was also lit by candles.

"I need a massage. I have had a long day," he said and laid on his stomach across the bed.

"I'm no licensed masseuse," Yvette said.

"Do you have some oil or lotion?"

"Yeah, look in the drawer over there." Yvette opened a drawer and retrieved a bottle of baby oil. She straddled Dalvin's back and begin to massage him. She massaged up and down his back.

"Damn that shit feels good," he moaned. "That's just what I needed."

He flipped over on his back, and threw Yvette off of him. She landed on her back, and he jumped on top of her. Apparently the massage charged him up like a battery. He was like an animal as he ripped off her underwear and snatched her shirt over her head. He bit into her neck and various parts of her body. It hurt but it felt good at the same time.

That night was a repeat of the first encounter and every other encounter afterwards. Each time it got better and better. All Dalvin had to do was text "WYA?" and Yvette was wherever he wanted her to be no matter the time of the day or night. She was addicted and needed that fix. She thought about him all the time. She pretty much fell in love with him without even trying or wanting to for that matter. She frequented Club Ignite on a regular, hoping to see him there. Sometimes she would call or text him offering to cook dinner at her place for him, but he never accepted the invitation. She thought she could handle it.

After each sexual rendezvous she never spent the night or fell asleep with him afterwards. She would shower and drive the distance home. She thought that by not laying with him afterwards, feelings would never be caught, but boy was she wrong. Somewhere in the midst of those sexual romps with Dalvin she lost her game face and was bitten. She even questioned if she ever had her game face on. She knew she had to shake the feeling but she couldn't. She took sexy photos and forwarded them to him. She wrote poetry about him. One was called "Me and Him."

Me and Him

I often sit around and I wonder if he thinks about me just as much as I think about me and him. I wonder if ......a smile crosses his lips like it does mine when I think about me and him. I wonder if....., he knows what a precious

Jewel he would have in his possession if it was just me and him. I wonder if... ..when he hears a love song like I do, if he thinks about me like I think about him, just daydreaming of me and him. I wonder if......he ever fantasize of walking down the aisle just me and him. I wonder if... ..,,he could imagine a love so Carefree just me and him. I wonder if... ,,,,,he knows, my very soul is set to fire at the very thought of me and him. I wonder if.....he could fathom the idea of my body shivering as if though cold at any glance shared between me and him. I wonder if......his heart flutters and his stomach becomes intertwined when he thinks of me and him. I wonder if...... the night we shared ever crosses his mind, his lips, his hands, all over my body when it was just me and him. I wonder if .....he wonders that I wonder about me and him. I wonder.......... Hmmmm, I just wonder....... if. And while I sit around and wonder if all these things I wonder will ever exist, he's probably not wondering, and could care less if there was ever a me and him.

He would only respond with one or two words like, "nice," or "looking good." Sometimes he would not respond at all, but that never changed what Yvette felt for him. His arrogance turned her on even more. It became a challenge for her to get him.

One Sunday evening just before dark, Yvette got the "WYA?" text from Dalvin and of course, she was wherever he wanted her to be. Usually that meant at his house. It wasn't quite dark when Yvette got to Dalvin's house this time. When she entered, there wasn't the usual lighted candles. Dalvin sat on the couch and watched Sunday football. This was different. Yvette had two glasses of Chardonnay before she got there and she was ready to go at it. Instead he wanted to finish watching the rest of the game.

"You want something to drink?" he asked.

"Yeah I do," she responded. Dalvin went into the kitchen to get her favorite, Chardonnay. She looked around his home. This was the first time she saw it in daylight. His decorating skills were on point for a man. It was adorned with family photos. There were photos of him at various concerts with artists and friends. One of the photos caused her to do a double-take. She looked and looked at one particular photo. She picked it up and stared hard. *This can't be* she thought. *My eyes must be playing tricks on me. Maybe I don't need another drink because I definitely must be drunk.*

On one of the pictures there was Dalvin and a group of guys at what look like an after-party. And there in that picture was none other than Geo! Yvette screamed on the inside. Dalvin came back with the glass of Chardonnay and went back to watching the end of the game. Yvette drank the glass of wine quickly, hoping to get so drunk she would forget what she saw. She knew it was him and it didn't matter if she drank the whole bottle. The picture would not change. Part of her wanted to get in her car and leave, but what excuse would she use? The other part of her wanted to feed her addiction so she decided to stay. After the game was over they went into Dalvin's room. Yvette couldn't get the vision of Dalvin and Geo out of her head. Was this a setup? What's really going on? *Was this Geo's way of getting back at me by allowing me to fall for his friend?* She decided to ask.

"Those guys in the photo at the after-party, are those friends of yours?"

"In one way or another, yes. I haven't seen some of them in years. Some have moved away. Others are still here, busy working, and we haven't had time to catch up," Dalvin said.

"How old is the picture?"

"May be five years old, why?"

"And you haven't seen or talked to any of them in five years?"

"Yeah, about that. Why are you asking all these questions about that one picture? Did you fuck one of them or something?" Dalvin asked.

"No why would you ask me that?" Yvette shouted.

"You seem overly curious about that one picture," he answered.

"I was asking because you say it's been five years, but the way you guys are dressed, it seems like ten years ago," Yvette laughed. "Just kidding," she said. "I need to use the restroom. I'll be back."

While in the restroom, Yvette cringed on the inside. She tried to think of an excuse to leave but what could she say? Yvette emerged from the restroom after having a quiet conniption and asked for another glass of wine. She figured if she got faded her mind would forget and she would enjoy the moment. In true Dalvin fashion, he gave her what she came for and it was good, but not quite the same. After it was over, she showered as usual, put her clothes on, and let herself out while Dalvin lay in bed on his stomach, fast asleep. On the way home, Yvette couldn't stop thinking, *this has got to be a set-up.*

A few weeks went by and Yvette was hit with the "WYD" text from Dalvin, to which she responded, "busy tonight."

Dalvin replied, "cool."

Yvette put some distance to the situation because she was conflicted by the photo. She could not stop feeling that something was not right.

She went about her weekly routine at work, going to the gym, then home to cook dinner for her young adults. She had taken a break from Club Ignite and from Dalvin for the moment. While doing laundry, a text notification went off on her phone.

The text read, "I still love you. I tried to move on with my life and I can't. I need to see you." She didn't recognize the number so she replied "who is this?"

"It's Geo," the text replied.

What in the hell? How could this be? Is this a coincidence? Now she really felt like this was a setup.

"Geo, I think it's best you move on with your life. Time has passed and I think it's best. I've moved on and you should, too," Yvette replied. The rejection must have made Geo angry.

His reply was, "Yeah bitch I heard you fucking a promoter now. I know him and I know people that know him and have seen you two together. Oh, by the way how is the new job going?" *How* does *he know these things?* Yvette thought.

"Look! Leave me alone. Don't text me anymore or I will get the police involved." There wasn't a reply. Yvette immediately got on the phone and called Dalvin.

"Hey Dalvin, I got a strange phone call from an ex of mine and he seems to know a few details about you and I. Can you please check your circle, and who you discuss us with, because I haven't spoke about our dealings and I find it odd that he would know what he knows."

Yvette never told Dalvin who her ex was or the fact that it happened to be a friend of his at some point or possibly still is.

"I don't need to talk to anyone. I never mention anything to anyone. You don't matter!" Dalvin responded.

Yvette's heart sank, like all of the air left her body. The words, "you don't matter," resonated loudly in her head.

Yvette hung up the phone. Hearing those words from him hurt her to the core of her being. Dalvin repeatedly tried to call Yvette back, but she never answered. No one had ever told her the hurt she felt that day, she wouldn't wish on her worst enemy.

At that moment she knew she had fallen in love for the first time in her life with a man who didn't give a damn about her. *I gave myself to him, I laid with him, I loved on him like a woman should. I thought that if I was attentive enough, was at his beck and call, received and gave back as much pleasure as he gave me, that maybe just maybe he would see me as more than just a fuck. I was a fool.* Yvette broke down and cried. She cried for hours. *Do I not matter? Is this why everything was going so wrong in my life. What's wrong with me*, she thought. Yvette began to question her looks, her weight, her body, everything about herself. *Why do I keep going down this road of destruction? All I ever wanted was a relationship that lasts. Ups and downs are a given as long as in the end you end up with a love that's forever.*

Yvette cried and fell to her knees. Yvette felt in her mind if she was strong enough, self-sufficient, kept her body tight and right, had a great career, and looked presentable at all times, she would be a great asset for any man, but apparently not. Yvette was not the player type. This whole "keep your game face on," "enjoy the moment as if nothing matters," was not her. As much as she had tried not to, she had fallen hard for Dalvin, a misogynistic fuck boy, indeed.

Days went by and Yvette still hurt from the words, "you don't matter." All she could think about was how much of a fool she was. He had basically showed her on more than one occasion that she didn't matter: the drives to his house that weren't reciprocated, the lack of return text messages. Over a year of sex, miles up and down the highway, trips to the club and hopes just to see his face, and from him nothing. *He's right, I don't matter and maybe just hearing it come from his mouth brought the truth and sometimes the truth hurts.*

CHAPTER 13
WOODEN NICKLES

Over a period of time the hurt lessened and Yvette was able to pull herself together. She still cared for Dalvin, she couldn't control it, but she came to terms with the fact that it would never be reciprocated, at least not the way she would have wanted it . And it did not mean something was wrong with her. Maybe it was him. After all, he was honest with her. Why did she think she could change that? First her husband, then Geo, now Dalvin. Each one of those relationships showed red flags from the beginning. Yvette finally understood what her grandma meant when she said, "Don't accept any wooden nickels." That simply meant, know what's real and what's not. No matter what someone tells you, don't let them convince you otherwise when you can clearly see it and know the difference. You're worth what's real and don't accept anything less. "Thanks, Grandma," Yvette said as she looked to the heavens. "I finally get it. It took me some time and some hurt but I finally get it."

One Saturday night her phone rang. It was Elisha.

"Bitch, it's time for you to climb out from under that rock, Let's hit Club Ignite!"

"Girl, I'm not trying to go there. I don't want to run into Dalvin. Why can't we find somewhere else to go?"

"All the more reasons why you should go. Show his ass you're unbothered. Show up and show out. Besides there's no other spot there's popping right now and you haven't been out in a while. You need to get out. Show him that you are not defeated by his player-ass bullshit."

"I don't know, let me think about it. I will call you later," Yvette said.

"Okay, at least you responded, but remember revenge is best served in a freakum dress, a pair of stilettos, hair on fleek, makeup done with a resting bitch face! I'm just saying."

Yvette laughed. "Girl, I will call you later, Bye." She lay in bed watching TV passing time and thinking. *I really should go and face him. I do need to get out the house, but what if I see him and I fall for him all over again? Or what if I see him and despise him?* Either way at some point she had to see him again. It was the only way to move forward.

She jumped up from the bed and decided to pull out her most scantily clad dress and platform stilettos. She texted Elisha and let her know she would meet her at the club around 9:30. She turned on Beyonce's song, "Get Me Bodied" and blasted it loud as she dressed. The dress was mid-thigh length, purple in color and backless. It was also sheer and see-through across the stomach and at the bottom above the knee.

The platform stilettos she wore were also purple and strappy. She flat-ironed her long black Brazilian weave that flowed down the middle of her back with side bangs that swept across her forehead and her perfectly beat to the gods makeup application. She took one last look in the mirror, grabbed her purse and keys, and out the door she went.

When she pulled up to Club Ignite, she felt an overwhelming sense of nervousness. *Did I over do it with a dress? Will I end up looking like I'm trying to get his attention instead of saying,* fuck you, I'm over it?"

She felt conflicted nevertheless she got out of the car determined to face her hurt. Once in the club she could see Elisha and Kelsey in their usual spot.

"Get it bitch!" Elisha shouted.

"Well push through then!" Kelsey said.

"You're not playing any games with that dress on. That's that fuck his head up dress!"

"No, it's not like that. I just want to have a good time. Besides I haven't been here in a minute," Yvette said. "I need something strong to drink." She ordered the club's infamous Long Island Iced Tea which was known to get some people drunk by only drinking one. She decided against her normal glass of Chardonnay. She wanted to get faded fast in case Dalvin showed up. Perhaps she would be numb. With the music blaring and drinks flowing, the trio made their way to the dance floor. Yvette forgot all about her hurt. She looked out into the crowd and spotted Mitchell. She hadn't seen him in a while. Once the songs changed, Yvette left the dance floor and went to say hello.

"Hi Mitch. What are you doing here, another party?"

"Hello stranger," Mitchell responded. "No, a buddy of mine is in town and I wanted to show him around. You're looking good."

"Thanks," she said and gave him a hug. She looked up from their embrace, and there was Dalvin. He had walked into the club at his usual 11 p.m. time. Many emotions ran through her mind. Among them were anger, hurt, and disappointment. Also somewhere among all of that she still felt some type of love for him. It wasn't the way she used to care about him, but something was still there. She walked back to the table where Kelsey and Elisha sat. But before she walked away he said, "I will be over there to get that dance you promised me last time."

"Okay," Yvette replied and continued to make her way to the table, but not before locking eyes with Dalvin. When she made it to the table, she made sure not to look in his direction and tried to avoid eye contact with him throughout the night. Later, Mitchell did come by and ask for the dance he was due. This time she did not hesitate to give him what she owed him. They made their way to the dance floor. Dalvin watched from the VIP section of the club where he normally sat. Yvette worked and danced with Mitchell while Dalvin stared. Actually, he wanted to make sure Yvette saw him staring. Nevertheless, she looked away and continue to dance. Once closing time came, Yvette agreed to hang out and eat with Mitchell. She never got a chance to say anything to Dalvin that night, or to tell him how he made her feel, so there wasn't any closure. However, she was able to let it go. the hurt wasn't to the degree it once was.

While eating, Yvette and Mitchell laughed and talked and caught up with each other lives since she had avoided him the whole time she was emotionally chained to Dalvin.

"Yvette, you know I really care about you, right?" We have been knowing each other for a while and I love you. I really do."

"Awwwww, Mitchell, I love you, too, Yvette responded.

Of course, she didn't think for once that he meant I love you in a literal sense. Yvette smiled and continued eating. Once they had finished eating, the two hugged and parted ways. On the way home, Yvette wished she would have gotten a chance to tell Dalvin how she felt. Meanwhile, Mitchell probably felt like, *Damn, I told her I love her and it went for nothing.*

CHAPTER 14
LETTING GO AND LETTING GOD

The new job was going great. Promotions and raises flowed freely. It seemed as if Yvette's life had finally taken a turn for the better. Yvette was promoted to senior VP of the company which came with a great salary. She had not received any more texts from Geo, and for the most part, Dalvin was finally out of her system. Her ex-husband started with his shoulda woulda coulda campaign, once more claiming that he wanted her back, but even with her unlucky relationships since their divorce, she could not fathom the idea of going backwards. She would have been a glutton for more punishment. Besides, once a cheater always a cheater.

Yvette put dating on hold and focused solely on her career. The children were out on their own. No more Club Ignite. She realized she needed a great deal of self-repair from everything that had happened. She needed a mental and physical cleansing of her mind, body, and soul. Everything was amazing. She didn't have a man in her life, but she didn't have any worries either. Yvette found a wonderful church home.

It was a beautiful Sunday afternoon and the church service was great. The Spirit of God was definitely high during service. She even got Kelsey and Elisha to attend.

"Girl, we should have been coming to church instead of clubbing, it's some fine brothers in here," Kelsey said looking around the congregation. "

"Stop! That's not the reason to come to church," Yvette responded.

"I couldn't do this on a regular basis. I mean it's okay to get your praise on once in a while but you know I got to get my life right before I start coming to church on a regular. I still got shit I like to do that God is not going to agree with," Elisha laughed.

"Why you got to cuss in church?" Yvette asked.

"See that's why I say I got to get my life right," Elisha said.

The trio proceeded to the parking lot to the car but continued to converse before they left.

"Girl that guy over there has been staring this way on and off since we've been standing in this parking lot," Kelsey mentioned.

"I hope he's not staring at me," Yvette said. "I hope he's staring at you. I have had enough dealing with these men. My focus is on me now and I don't want to be bothered. He's walking this way so we will find out."

"Good afternoon, ladies," the tall, handsome fair-skinned gentleman spoke. "I'm Joseph. I'm new to the area and church. I wanted to introduce myself to some of the members and ask a few questions about the inner-workings of the church."

"We are not members," Kelsey said, "but our friend, Yvette, here is a member."

Kelsey pushed Yvette forward.

"I couldn't tell you much about the inner-workings because I'm fairly new myself. But I will say the pastor is phenomenal and the choir is amazing. You will most definitely get the word one way or the other," Yvette said.

"I most certainly enjoyed the service today. Maybe we can get together for brunch next Sunday after service and chat about it and you can tell me all about the other happening spots here," Joseph smiled. His beautiful white teeth were surrounded by a pair of slightly full lips, skin the color of honey. Dreadlocks adorned his head and lay down his back.

He was a far cry from a guy Yvette would be attracted to. Joseph had strategically-placed freckles, and wore a basic button-down long-sleeve shirt, slacks, and a tie. He definitely was not her norm, which is why she agreed to brunch. She knew nothing would come of it because the attraction was not there, at least not for her.

"Sure, that sounds great."

"I will see you next Sunday. Ladies, nice to meet you." Joseph flashed a pearly white smile and he walked to his car.

"He's hot," Elisha said.

"You think all men are hot," Kelsey replied.

"Girl, I'm not interested. It's a church thing. I'm going to have brunch and swap insights on the church," Yvette said.

"Swap insights, huh?" Kelsey laughed.

"Why does everything have to be so sexual with y'all? Jesus!" Yvette shouted. "He's not my type."

Next Sunday came and went. Brunch with Joseph was actually nice. He was quite the gentleman. He made Yvette laugh and conversation flowed effortlessly. In time, they even talked on the phone here and there and when they did talk, they talk for hours. It was incredible how much they had in common. Joseph asked Yvette out on a couple of dates that included the movies, dinner, and bowling. Each date they had an amazing time. Yvette actually enjoyed the fact that they had an amazing time with no strings, drama, or sex attached.

About a month into it while having their usual conversation, Joseph asked, "What are you looking for?"

"What do you mean?" Yvette asked.

"You know what I mean, as for a man in your life right now." Joseph replied.

"I'm really not looking for anything. It's been two years since my last relationship and I'm okay with that."

"I want to be married," Joseph said. "I'm at the age where I have done all the clubbing and have had all the sexual experiences I want. Now I want something more, something that's for me and for me only, I want a wife."

"I've been there and done that."

"So you're saying you wouldn't get married again?" Joseph asked.

"I'm not saying that. I'm saying it would probably take a lot though."

"You shouldn't let what one man did, deter you from allowing the right man to be everything you need and more." It wasn't just one, it was a few," Yvette chuckled.

"But I've learned a lot and it has made me stronger."

"Made you stronger, or caused you to build a wall," Joseph asked. "Let me pose a question to you differently. What is it that you need and want from a man?"

"All I ask is for consistency, honesty, and love," Yvette replied.

"That's it? If that's all you want, you're not asking for much," Joseph said.

"You think so? Tell that to the men of the world today, and it seems to be like a child on the back of a milk carton, missing."

Joseph laughed. "Now that was funny. At least pull that wall down to your chin and give someone else a chance to work on the rest." Yvette smiled. *Where do I go from here she thought.* Dates and conversations between Joseph and Yvette continued without sexual undertones, just two people enjoying each other's company. Although he wasn't Yvette's usual type, Joseph started to grow on her. She started to find several things about him that she was attracted to that had been overshadowed by what she thought she was attracted to. Steven had invited Yvette out often and always insisted on paying. Yvette wanted to do something nice to show her appreciation so she decided to have him over for dinner.

"Hey, Joseph. I was wondering if you would like to come over for dinner."

"You cook?"

"Yes, I cook, why do you seem surprised?"

"I'm not talking about Hamburger Helper," he laughed.

"Excuse you! I can cook!" Yvette replied.

"Just kidding. I would love to."

"Okay, be at my house around 8."

"I will see you at 8."

"That night, Yvette prepared baked chicken, rice pilaf and steamed veggies. She had also chilled a bottle of red wine and made a fruit medley for dessert. Dinner was healthy and delicious.

"Thanks for inviting me," Joseph said.

"You're welcome." They retire to the sofa with their glasses of wine to relax. They listened to music and used their conversation to unwind. As the wine glass kept getting refilled and the music continue to play, the conversation got deeper.

"Yvette, you are one beautiful and sexy woman. I've wanted to say that all night."

"Thank you," Yvette responded. Joseph leaned in to kiss Yvette and she pulled away.

"What's wrong?" he asked.

"Look, Joseph. We're having a good time. I've been having a good time with you. I don't want to tarnish that."

"Why would it," he asked. "Yvette, I'm not them, and I want more. I want to be more than just your friend. I honestly want a wife. I'm not sure if you're her, but I know I like you a lot and I want to be with you. I want to be yours," Joseph said.

With disdain, Yvette responded, "Just say you want to fuck, damn! We've been hanging out for a couple of months and you want to fuck. That was a nice way to say it though."

"Why are you talking to me like that?" Joseph asked.

"You're no different, you just waited longer."

"What are you talking about? Yvette, I genuinely like and care about you more than you know."

"Whatever!" Yvette replied. At that Joseph got up and walked towards the door.

"I think I'm going to leave now."

"Why, because I'm right?" Yvette asked.

"No, because you disrespected my feelings."

"Disrespected your feelings?" Yvette shouted.

Joseph opened the door and but before he left, he

turned to Yvette and said, "You're so used to fighting, but I guarantee you if you give the right man half a chance you will never have to fight again, at least not the way you've had to fight. He will fight with you. You'll never have to fight alone and the fight will always be worth it."

Yvette couldn't say a word.

"Thanks for dinner. He kissed her on the forehead and turned and walked out the door.

"Wait, Joseph. I apologize. It's so hard for me to take men seriously these days with everything I've been through. I don't want to go down that road again." He looked her in the eyes and cupped her chin in his hands.

"I'm not them." She invited Steven back in and they continue the evening with a movie on Netflix. Yvette relaxed enough to allow herself to lay in his arms and watch the movie. The two ended up falling asleep. Yvette got up to use the restroom. Joseph clutched her around her waist and pulled her towards him to resume cuddling.

"I'm just going to the restroom. I'm coming back," she whispered. He released his grip. When she came back to resume cuddling, she watched Joseph for a minute as he slept peacefully. He looked very handsome. She positioned herself back on his chest and began to rub her hands across his chest. She traced his facial features softly with her fingertips. Joseph awakened, looked at Yvette, smiled, and kissed her softly. That started the beginning of a beautiful sexual session. Steven took his time and caressed every part of Yvette's body.

"You sure you want to do this?" he asked. "We don't have to do this. I want all of you, not just this and I can wait.

"I'm sure," Yvette replied. In that instance, Joseph began a whirl-wind of sexual ecstasy that took Yvette's breath away. It was like none of her other sexual escapades. This felt like love was involved. The way he took his time with her, leaving no parts of her body untouched by passionate kisses. He left her very satisfied. Yvette felt like she had finally found a man to break those soul ties. He was amazing. Time went on and things remained the same. Their talks continued and they grew closer and closer. Yvette had unexpectedly fallen in love against everything she had said, and it felt amazing. Every so often she did find herself comparing the sexual experiences in her past to the one that she was in now. *Snap out of it* she told herself. This man is amazing. You have kissed a million frogs and now you have found your prince. The love they experienced was on top! Later that day Joseph called Kelsey.

"Hey, Kelsey is Joseph. I know you're wondering how I got your number but I got it out of Yvette's phone."

"Oh, hey, Joseph, what's up?"

"Look, you know how much I love Yvette, right?"

"I do now," Kelsey laughed.

"I want her to be my wife. I want to propose and I need help planning it."

"Oh, my God!" Kelsey shouted. "Are you serious?"

"Yes, I'm serious. I knew when I saw her in the church parking lot, she was it."

"Yes, of course I will help you," Kelsey said.

Over the course of a few weeks, Joseph and Kelsey worked hard behind Yvette's back. They were careful so that she did not suspect anything. Kelsey and Elisha planned for the proposal to take place at Club Ignite. Joseph would come out during the band session and propose.

One Saturday night, against everything Yvette felt, the dynamic duo manged to get Yvette to the club after much begging and pleading. She hope that she would not see Dalvin. It was her prayer that maybe he would be off promoting a concert or something. Another part of her hoped that maybe he would be there. It was the only way she would know if the hold was truly broken now that she was in love with Joseph. The three ladies sat in their usual area of the club. Music was was usually played by a DJ but on this particular night a band provided live entertainment. The band sounded amazing. It was a pleasant change.

One of the performers stepped to the microphone and said, "Okay, we're going to slow this thing down for the lovers and the steppers."

The song, by an artist called K'Jon, played. Yvette loved this song. Kelsey knew that was the cue. Of course she waited to share the news with Elisha because then the whole world would have known, if she had told her prior to today. So, she was clueless about the proposal. As the band continue to play, the ladies moved and sway to the music. Yvette felt a tap on her shoulder and almost dreaded turning around out of fear that would be Dalvin. She took a deep breath and turned around and it was Joseph, suited and booted down on one knee with a diamond ring fit for a queen. The music from the band lowered as Joseph began to speak.

"Yvette from the moment I laid eyes on you, I knew you were it for me and my search was over. If you accept this proposal, I promise you, you would never have to fight alone again. I want you to rest and let me fight for you. Will you please do me the honor of being my wife? Will you marry me?"

Yvette was already sobbing and she answered with a resounding, "yes," and quickly jumped into her future husband's arms. As she wiped away her tears she looked to one side of the room to see Mitchell standing with a disappointed look on his face and Dalvin in his usual spot looking devious. Nevertheless, she was about to marry a man who loved her wholeheartedly and she loved him.

CHAPTER 15
THE BEGINNING OR THE END?

The following year, Yvette found herself in a marathon race to finish odds and ends in preparation for the big day. The wedding was only a couple of days away. It was down to the finalization of the decorations for the venue, dress fittings, rehearsals, and dinners. Yvette finally found some quiet time to sit down and reflect on her life. all of The pain and anguish that ensued from the abundance of emotional turmoil and the wreckage that could have literally took her out mentally and physically. However, she overcame and pushed through by the grace of God. She also thought about the look on Mitchell's and Dalvin's face the night of the proposal. After all, she had cut him off and stopped talking to him knowing how much he cared for her. Yvette decided to drive over to the gun range and see him face to face and apologize.

Mitchell's receptionist called him in his office to let him know that he had a visitor.

"Yvette, what are you doing here? Shouldn't you be somewhere getting ready for your big day?"

"Mitchell, I wanted to come by and see you before everything went down. I wanted to thank you for always being there for me and to let you know I'm sorry for cutting you off like that."

"Yvette, I love you, and I always will. I want you to be happy even if it's not with me. I'll always be here for you if you need me."

"That means a lot to me, Mitchell, thanks."

She hugged him and turned to walk away with him still holding on to her hand like he didn't want to let go. Yvette turned and looked at Mitchell and smiled. He smiled back and let her hand go. Dalvin crossed her mind but she didn't feel like she owed him any explanation or an apology. It It is what it is. After all, she didn't matter, that's what he said. Even though the times they shared were incredibly indescribable, those three words would take a long time to heal from.

The time finally came for Yvette to become Mrs. Joseph Jennings. Yvette chose an outdoor venue with landscaped grounds, a classic European formal garden and a beautiful pond with a wooden row boat, huge overgrown trees and a water fountain. It was a beautiful day in April. Flowers were everywhere.

The day was perfect to get married. Shades of purple and seafoam green décor and flowers with a hint of silver adorned the venue. Drones flew overhead to capture every moment. Yvette and her bride's court waited inside a beautiful limestone building for the coordinator to give them their cue, while Joseph and his groomsmen patiently wait at the altar. The bridesmaids and other members of the bridal party filed out one by one until only Yvette was left standing there with her dad. It was extremely important for him to be there. He wasn't able to attend her first marriage due to illness, so his brother stood in for him.

The time came for her to walk out and become a wife again and she prayed it would be her last time. With her father by her side, the song, "One in a Million You" by Larry Graham played in the background. Yvette walked out to see her handsome groom. He waited with a smile that showed his one dimple like he had won the lottery. Yvette's stomach was in knots. She did everything she could not to cry and mess up her makeup. With each step, the words in the song resonated deeply with her. Soon it became impossible to hold back tears. As the song played on, there wasn't a dry eye in the house. Yvette made her way to the altar, where Kelsey and Elisha stood as her bridesmaid and matron of honor. Joseph looked like the king he was with nothing but love and admiration in his eyes. His dreads were neatly pinned back and draped down his back.

"Who gives this woman to this man?" the pastor asked.

"I do," Yvette's father replied, kissed Yvette on the cheek and handed her off to Joseph. Joseph and Yvette stood hand-in-hand and face-to-face looking deep into each other's eyes.

"Is there anyone here with just purpose why these two should not be joined in holy matrimony, let them speak now or forever hold their peace," the pastor continued. The venue was quiet.

The pastor cleared his throat to continue with the ceremony, but before he could begin a voice cried out from a distance, "Yvette! Yvette, I love you!" She turned around to see where the voice was coming from, and so did everyone else. Yvette could not believe it! How could he?

ABOUT THE AUTHOR

Y. R. Perry, was born in California, but currently resides in Texas. She is a talented hair stylist, makeup artist, mother and now author. Journaling over the years became her solace so much she decided to use her creative writing skills and pour into her passion for writing and produce her first of three novels, *Tumultuous, Tumultuous Too…* the sequel and *Tumultuous, the Apogee.* Enjoy…..

www.ingramcontent.com/pod-product-compliance
Lightning Source LLC
Chambersburg PA
CBHW032054150426
43194CB00006B/524